The Battleship Potemkin

KINOfiles Film Companions

General Editor: Richard Taylor

Written for cineastes and students alike, KINOfiles are readable, authoritative, illustrated companion handbooks to the most important and interesting films to emerge from Russian cinema from its beginnings to the present. Each KINOfile investigates the production, context and reception of the film and the people who made it, and analyses the film itself and its place in Russian and World cinema. KINOfiles will also include films of the other countries that once formed part of the Soviet Union, as well as works by émigré film-makers working in the Russian tradition.

KINOfiles form a part of KINO: The Russian Cinema Series.

THE BATTLESHIP POTEMKIN

The Film Companion

RICHARD TAYLOR

KINOfiles Film Companion 1

I.B.Tauris *Publishers*
LONDON • NEW YORK

Published in 2000 by I.B.Tauris & Co Ltd
Victoria House, Bloomsbury Square, London WC1B 4DZ
175 Fifth Avenue, New York NY 10010
www.ibtauris.com

In the United States of America and in Canada distributed by
St Martins Press, 175 Fifth Avenue, New York NY 10010

ISBN 1 86064 393 0

A full CIP record for this book is available from the British Library
A full CIP record for this book is available from the Library of Congress

Library of Congress catalog card: available

Typeset in Monotype Calisto by the Midlands Book Typesetting Company,
Loughborough, Leicestershire
Printed and bound in Great Britain by MPG Books Ltd, Bodmin, Cornwall

This book is dedicated to Jeffrey Richards, scholar, gentleman and wit, in fraternal gratitude for more than thirty-five years of friendship.

'The battleship is alive and breathing as a mighty mutinous collective – all for one and one for all! This film will be studied for a long time and a commentary on it – on almost every shot – could even now, at first impression, constitute a whole book.'

Vladimir Blium, '*Bronenosets Potemkin*', *Izvestiia*, February 1926, no. 19.

Contents

List of Illustrations

Acknowledgements

Apart from the usual genuine and heartfelt acknowledgements to family and friends, I should like to thank the following for their particular help and encouragement in the eventual completion of this project: above all Julian Graffy, who read part of the manuscript at an early stage and made his usual valuable comments; Birgit Beumers, Graham Roberts and Philippa Brewster, for their exemplary patience while my dilatoriness delayed the launch of the KINOfile series; and Naum Kleiman, Oksana Bulgakowa, Ekaterina Khokhlova, Jeffrey Richards, Howell Davies, Richard Shannon, Peter Matthews, Neil Harding and Eleanor Breuning, for clarifying various detailed points. I should also like to thank the University of Wales Swansea for generous financial and practical support.

The illustrations in this book come from my own collection.

Richard Taylor
Swansea, St David's Day 2000

Note on Transliteration

Transliteration from the Cyrillic to the Latin alphabet is a perennial problem for writers on Russian subjects. I have opted for a dual system: in the text I have used the Library of Congress system (without diacritics), but I have broken from this system (a) when a Russian name has a clear English version (e.g. Maria instead of Mariia, Alexander instead of Aleksandr); (b) when a Russian name has an accepted English spelling, or when Russian names are of Germanic origin (e.g. Yeltsin instead of Eltsin; Eisenstein instead of Eizenshtein); (c) when a Russian surname ends in -ii or -yi this is replaced by a single -y (e.g. Dostoevsky instead of Dostoevskii), and all Christian names end in a single -i. In the scholarly apparatus I have adhered to the Library of Congress system (with diacritics) for the specialist.

Credits

The Battleship Potemkin [Bronenosets Potemkin]

Production:

Director:	Sergei M. Eisenstein [Eizenshtein]
Script:	Sergei M. Eisenstein, from an idea by Nina F. Agadzhanova-Shutko
Photography:	Eduard K. Tisse
Camera assistant:	Vladimir Popov
Assistant director:	Grigori V. Alexandrov
Assistants (the 'iron five'):	Grigori V. Alexandrov (assistant director)
	Alexander P. Antonov
	Mikhail Gomorov
	Alexander I. Lyovshin
	Maxim M. Strauch [Shtraukh]
Editing:	Sergei M. Eisenstein
Art direction:	Vasili A. Rakhals
Intertitles:	Nikolai N. Aseev, in collaboration with Sergei M. Tretiakov
Music (for German release):	Edmund Meisel
Producer:	Iakov M. Bliokh

Cast:

Vakulinchuk, a sailor	Alexander P. Antonov
Captain Golikov	Vladimir G. Barsky
Chief Officer Giliarovsky	Grigori V. Alexandrov

Petty Officer	Alexander I. Liovshin
Matiushenko,	
a non-commissioned officer	Mikhail Gomorov
Boatswain	Nikolai Levchenko
Officer	Marusov
Recruits	I. Bobrov, Andrei A. Fait
Woman on the Odessa	
Steps	Beatrice Vitoldi
Woman with pince-nez	
on the Odessa Steps	N. Poltavtseva
Woman weeping in front	
of Vakulinchuk's tent	Repnikova
Woman bringing food	
for the crew	Iulia Eisenstein
Other cast members	Sailors of the Red Navy;
	citizens of Odessa;
	members of the Proletkult Theatre,
	Moscow
Production:	First Goskino Factory, Moscow
Original length:	5 reels, 1,820 metres
First showing:	21 December 1925, Bolshoi
	Theatre, Moscow
Release date:	18 January 1926, Moscow

1. Production History

The Battleship Potemkin was originally conceived as one episode in a series of films celebrating the anniversary of the revolutionary events of 1905 under the generic title, The Year 1905 [1905 god].[1] The film was contracted on 17 March 1925 by the Government Commission established to commemorate the twentieth anniversary in 1925.[2] The composition of the Commission is worth noting. It was chaired by the People's Commissar for Enlightenment, Anatoli Lunacharsky, who had a reputation for being an intellectual among the Bolsheviks and a Bolshevik among the intellectuals. The other members included: Kazimir Malevich, the Suprematist artist; Vsevolod Meyerhold, the innovative theatre director whom Eisenstein subsequently referred to as 'my spiritual father';[3] Valerian Pletniov, representing the radical proletarian culture movement, Proletkult; Kirill Shutko, from the Party's Agitprop Department;[4] Leonid Krasin, a member of the Party Central Committee; and Vasili Mikhailov, the First Secretary of the Moscow City Party.

The original intention was for The Year 1905 to be based on a treatment written by Nina Agadzhanova-Shutko (the wife of Kirill, an Old Bolshevik in her own right and author of the successful script for the film Behind White Lines [V tylu u belykh, dir. B. Chaikovsky and O. Rakhmanova, 1924]), Eisenstein and Valerian Pletniov. The two men had collaborated, as fellow members of Proletkult, on the script for Eisenstein's first feature-length film – the highly experimental The Strike [Stachka, 1924] – but had subsequently fallen out over the attribution of the authorship of the script to the Proletkult collective as a whole. After a barbed exchange of letters Eisenstein had left the Proletkult movement altogether.[5] Since neither Eisenstein nor Pletniov wished to renew their acquaintance, Pletniov dropped out of the project, and Nuné (as Eisenstein called her) was left to draft the script.[6]

1. Eisenstein and his film crew, Sebastopol

In its original version the project was to provide a panoramic coverage of the most important events of 1905 from the Russo-Japanese War and the Bloody Sunday massacre in January to the tsar's manifesto establishing the Duma, the widespread strikes and the fighting on the barricades. Eisenstein later argued that 'I had my own principled demands of the script: the absence of central heroic characters, an emphasis on the mass, on collective action, and so on.'[7] When the Government Commission met again on 4 June 1925 it became clear that *The Year 1905* was to constitute only one part of an ambitious programme of celebrations for the anniversary. Malevich was put in charge of the visual aspects of the celebrations, while Meyerhold, during his forthcoming foreign trip, was to approach Sergei Prokofiev and try to persuade him to return to the Soviet Union and compose a commemorative symphony to accompany the film.[8] This mission represents a curious foretaste of the later collaboration between composer and film-maker on both *Alexander Nevsky* [1938] and the two completed parts of *Ivan the Terrible*. As Eisenstein later recalled, 'The lofty peaks of musical genius and bureaucracy could not be reconciled. And I had the good fortune to share in this notable man's creativity many years later. In 1925 we only dreamed about this.'[9]

Because of the vast scale of the film project, the Commission envisaged from the very beginning that only *one* episode in the epic panorama would actually be completed in time for the anniversary celebrations on 20 December 1925, with the rest of the series completed as late as August 1926. This episode would cover the October strike in St Petersburg with the mutiny on the 'Potemkin' as a brief prologue.[10] But permission for even this episode to go into production was not given until June 1925.[11]

Eisenstein, Nuné and Grigori Alexandrov, Eisenstein's assistant, worked on the script for *The Year 1905* throughout the spring and summer of 1925. For this purpose they were given use of the Shutkos' dacha at Nemchinovka on the outskirts of Moscow. The Shutkos shared the dacha with Malevich and his second wife, who owned it. The writer Isaak Babel also joined them. In order to accept the important anniversary commission, Eisenstein had had to abandon his planned film version of Babel's *Red Cavalry* [Konarmiia] stories. Nonetheless the two were still determined to collaborate on a film project, *Benya Krik*, based on Babel's stories of Jewish life in Odessa, and Eisenstein spent part of each day working with Nuné on *1905* and part with Babel on *Benya Krik*. The seed of Odessa was thus already planted before Eisenstein visited the city: the Babel adaptation never came to fruition but the influence can be seen in *Potemkin*.

The Goskino studio had envisaged 250 days for the shooting with a cast of 20,000. In a newspaper interview in July 1925 Eisenstein remarked that 'The production of *The Year 1905* should be on a grandiose scale like the German film *The Nibelungs*.'[12] Shooting was originally envisaged all over the country but began in Moscow. At the beginning of August 1925 Eisenstein travelled to Leningrad, formerly the imperial capital St Petersburg, to shoot with 700 extras the scenes of the general strike that had led to the Tsar's manifesto of 17 October 1905 conceding the establishment of the State Duma. However it rained incessantly so that the natural light was too weak for filming and the lighting technology of the time (which included the use of naval searchlights) required so much energy that the whole city had regularly to be plunged into darkness. Furthermore, Eisenstein's usual cameraman, Eduard Tisse, was filming elsewhere and the substitute, Alexander Levitsky, while experienced, was also afraid of heights and did not like filming from the rooftops.

Moreover, the original intention had been to film the (eventually final) scene where 'Potemkin' sails to meet the fleet in the Baltic, rather than the Black Sea, but the Baltic Fleet had already left port.

Eisenstein's assistant and life-long friend, Maxim Strauch, followed them to Kronstadt, where they declined to be filmed and suggested using the Black Sea Fleet, whose ships were more similar to the original 'Potemkin', instead.[13] At the same time, the Goskino studio director, Mikhail Kapchinsky, whom Strauch later described as 'our guardian angel', advised Eisenstein not to endanger the whole project by persevering in Leningrad, but to travel south to film in Odessa, where at least the sun was shining and filming could begin on both the printers' strike there and the 'Potemkin' mutiny. Odessa also happened to be Kapchinsky's home town and he said that he could vouch for the weather! The film crew left the shores of the Baltic in mid-August and arrived on the shores of the Black Sea on 24 August 1925.

Maxim Strauch recollects that, while they were filming in Moscow, he had been working in the library to gather material for the film and had come across a drawing in the French journal *L Illustration* of shooting on the Odessa Steps. He had shown this picture to Eisenstein and it had stimulated childhood memories of a similar incident in Riga. When they arrived in Odessa, according to Strauch, they went straight to the Odessa Steps, without stopping for breakfast.[14] Nonetheless, while the weather seemed to have decided the question of which episode of *The Year 1905* would be finished in time for the anniversary celebrations, Eisenstein clearly had not. He hesitated, as he was to hesitate a decade later over *Bezhin Meadow* [Bezhin lug, 1935–7], and, instead of filming, busied himself with writing a fuller script for the *Potemkin* episode, including the Odessa Steps sequence, which had not featured in Nuné's original script for *The Year 1905*. The crew remained idle while the first mists of late summer descended on the port. Levitsky the cameraman, who had fallen ill, tired of waiting and left. Eisenstein sent Alexandrov to Moscow to persuade Tisse to return with him and the pair arrived in Odessa by 23 September. Tisse was prepared to film in the misty conditions and shooting started again on 28 September. The lyrical mist-laden scenes of the port of Odessa were shot during a boat trip round the harbour taken by Eisenstein, Tisse and Alexandrov and were not originally intended for inclusion in the film.[15] When she saw the rough cuts of these sequences Nuné wrote to Eisenstein, 'Tisse is not a cameraman – he is God.'[16]

Contrary to a widely held belief, not all the roles in *Potemkin* were played by amateurs who merely 'looked the type'. Two of Eisenstein's Proletkult colleagues played leading roles: his assistant, Grigori Alexandrov, played the officer-villain Giliarovsky while Alexander

2. Filming the Odessa Steps: Eisenstein and his 'iron five'

Antonov, by contrast, played the sailor-hero Vakulinchuk. On the
other hand, the role of Captain Golikov went to the director Vladimir
Barsky, who just happened to be filming his *The Highest Wave*
[Deviatyi val, 1926] in Odessa and who, in Eisenstein's view, 'looked
the part'.[17] Doctor Smirnov, who turned his blind pince-nez to the

rotten meat, the priest and the majority of the smaller and bit parts were also cast in accordance with the basic principle of 'typage' (*tipazh*), namely that they quite simply looked right for the part as Eisenstein envisaged it. The following advertisement appeared in one of the Odessa papers:

For the shooting of the anniversary film *The Year 1905* (director S. Eisenstein) we require models [*naturshchiki*] with the following characteristics:

1 Woman of about 27, Jewess, brunette, tall, thinnish, spirited (for the scene with the Bundiste).
2 Man, aged 30–40, tall, broad-shouldered, physically very strong, good-natured open Russian face, an 'uncle' figure like the German actor Emil Jannings.
3 Man, height and age unimportant, average drunkard type, insolent facial expression, flaxen-haired, defect in the arrangement of the eyes desirable (slight squint, eyes too far apart, etc.)[18]

This advertisement makes clear the detail with which Eisenstein defined his 'types'. External appearance and demeanour were the criteria by which the roles were filled, whether by professional actors or amateurs.

The sequence that lies at the heart of *Potemkin*, the massacre on the Odessa Steps, took two weeks to film. Eisenstein was not the first film director to use the 120 steps in this way: in 1922 Vladimir Gardin, veteran director and first head of the State Film School, re-created a massacre on the same spot for his film *A Spectre Is Haunting Europe* [Prizrak brodit po Evrope, 1923].[19] Gardin's film was a screen adaptation of Edgar Allan Poe's depiction of revolutionary upheaval, *The Masque of the Red Death*, and was released by the Yalta branch of the VUFKU [All-Ukrainian Photo-Cine Enterprise] studio, whose films were not normally widely distributed outside the Ukraine. However the film *was* reviewed in both *Pravda* and *Izvestiia* at the time of its release and, although Gardin was hardly a popular director with the avant-garde, his film may at least have made Eisenstein aware of the possibilities that Odessa offered as a suitable location for a massacre.[20] One-tenth of the footage of the Odessa Steps sequence in *Potemkin* was shot without a tripod. The camera team were lowered over wooden platforms by means of boards and ropes. On occasion they had in effect to abseil down the steps to be caught by their colleagues below.

3. *Potemkin*: typical typage types

4. Eisenstein and crew, Odessa

The crowd was kept in check by the 'iron five' – Eisenstein's assistants (Grigori Alexandrov, Maxim Strauch, Mikhail Gomorov, Alexander Antonov and Alexander Liovshin) all dressed in striped shirts, with the aid of a 35-man brass band.[21]

Once the Odessa Steps massacre had been filmed, the crew left for Sebastopol to film the shipboard scenes. The original battleship 'Potemkin' had been decommissioned in 1919 and broken up, but its sister ship 'The Twelve Apostles' was still at anchor off the Crimea. Unfortunately it was being used to store mines and this severely limited the film crew's room for manoeuvre. For these reasons only the quarterdeck sequences were filmed on 'The Twelve Apostles', while the below-deck filming took place on another ship, the 'Comintern', to avoid the danger of a fatal explosion.[22] Tisse claimed that some of the shooting had to be done in the middle of a force 9 gale and that he and his camera had to be held secure by six other men.[23] Eisenstein later remarked that 'Russians can overcome any obstacle.'[24] These difficulties meant that it took a month to shoot the scene with the rotten meat – twice as long as for the Odessa Steps sequence, which lasted six times as long on screen. The original intention had

Eisenstein's 'iron five': from bottom to top, Grigori Alexandrov, Maxim Strauch, Mikhail Gomorov, Alexander Antonov, Alexander Liovshin

been to complete all the shooting in Odessa and Sebastopol in fifteen days but it eventually took 54 days. The scenes of mass mourning in Odessa were all shot in a single day, while filming the skiffs in Sebastopol took only four hours. The sailors in the mutiny scene on the quarterdeck and elsewhere were all sailors in real life and their discipline was vital in completing the shooting in such difficult circumstances.[25] As Eisenstein later observed in his memoirs, 'The implacable constraints of space kept us in check. The deadlines were no less implacable. We had to deliver the picture on the anniversary, and that concentrated the mind wonderfully.'[26]

The director and his 'iron five' had to act as stuntmen for the dangerous sequences: Eisenstein himself donned the priest's garb for the fall down the gangway, because the gardener who was playing the part declined to do anything so dangerous.[27] The others dressed in officer's uniform to dive into the sea after the mutineers had captured the battleship. On a day off from normal shooting Eisenstein, Alexandrov, Strauch and Tisse went sightseeing to the former governor's palace at Alupka, in the Crimea. As a souvenir of their visit they filmed the three stone lions – asleep, half-awake, and leaping to its feet – that they were later to employ as a symbol of popular revolutionary awakening.[28]

By 23 November the time had come for Eisenstein to return to Moscow: he now had 4,500 metres with which to make the finished film and less than a month in which to do it. He still had to shoot the scenes of the model battleship floating in the city's Sandunov baths.[29] The shots of the squadron in the final part of the film were taken from a World War I newsreel: some accounts suggest that the footage in fact depicts the Royal Navy but this has never been confirmed. All these constraints at last persuaded Eisenstein that, if the film were to be finished in time for the December anniversary celebrations, he would have to jettison the coverage of the October strike and concentrate on the mutiny on the battleship, which in Nuné's original script had occupied only 44 shots out of a total of 820, compared with 655 in Eisenstein's finished film.[30] It was therefore only at this late stage, less than one month before its premiere, that *The Year 1905* finally became *The Battleship Potemkin*. This late conversion to the idea that made Eisenstein famous is confirmed by contemporary press reports which, right up until the last minute, referred to the forthcoming film as *The Year 1905*. In an article in November 1925, the scriptwriter's husband, Kirill Shutko, claimed that 'The script for the film was supposed to provide the skeleton for the selection of the raw material and its internal organization. The details, the emphases remained the director's responsibility.'[31]

Meanwhile, back in the south Alexandrov and Tisse filmed the remaining parts of the final confrontation, and some final shots of the

Odessa Steps sequence, without the director.[32] This gave rise to the claim that it was actually Tisse and not Eisenstein who directed the film. There is no credible evidence for this, and in fact Alexandrov sent detailed daily reports of the shooting to Eisenstein in Moscow, which he would obviously not have thought necessary had Tisse in fact been the director.

Eisenstein had three weeks to turn more than 4,500 metres of film into the finished version of around 1,850 metres. It was no mean task and *The Battleship Potemkin* was only barely ready for the premiere in the Bolshoi Theatre on 21 December 1925, the day after the anniversary. The rough cut had 1,280 takes. As Tisse carried the first reels of the film into the projection box at the Bolshoi, Eisenstein was still sticking the last reels together in the cutting room, so that Alexandrov had to ferry them to the theatre on his motorbike. The director later recalled his growing fears of impending disaster:

> In the rush in the editing suite we had omitted to glue the end of the last part of the film together. To stop them from flying apart and being mixed up, I had stuck them together with spit ... And then I distinctly remembered: the editors did not have time to glue the final version. The one which had already been wound on to the spool ... The film would come apart at any moment! The projector would send fragments flying ... The rhythm of the film's finale would be broken. And suddenly, imagine! A miracle! The spit held.[33]

This first performance, which Eisenstein called this 'miracle in the Bolshoi Theatre', was thus very much a rough-cut version. The theatre orchestra, used to accompanying classical opera and ballet, had gone on strike demanding to know what sort of music they were expected to play for the rotten meat sequence. In the end the accompaniment consisted of a medley of tunes from Litolff's 'Robespierre' overture, Beethoven's 'Egmont' overture and Tchaikovsky's symphonic fantasia 'Francesca da Rimini', music familiar to the orchestra but perhaps not entirely appropriate to such an avant-garde film, even if the two overtures apparently had the right ideological credentials. It had also been Eisenstein's original idea that in the closing sequence, as the prow of the battleship cuts the screen in half, the screen should actually be torn in two revealing a group of real 'Potemkin' sailors on the stage. This idea of introducing such a theatrical live-action device was, not surprisingly, abandoned.

As we shall see when we deal with the reception of the film, *Potemkin* catapulted its 27-year-old director to international prominence. But the master copy of the film was treated in a way that no major work in any other art form would be treated. In 1926 the negative was sold to Germany because the Soviet Union did not have the technological capability to duplicate it. The negative was cut in accordance with the demands of the German censorship authorities, the off-cuts lost and the censored negative sold back to the Soviet cinema authorities in 1940 at the time of the Nazi-Soviet Pact.[34] That is why there is no unquestionably authentic copy of the film in existence today.

Notes

In these and subsequent notes the following abbreviations have been used for frequently cited sources: full details can be found in the section on *Further Reading*:

ER:	*The Eisenstein Reader*
ESW1:	Eisenstein, *Selected Works*, vol. 1
ESW4:	Eisenstein, *Selected Works*, vol. 4
FF:	R. Taylor & I. Christie (eds), *The Film Factory.*
K&L	N. Kleiman & K. Levina (eds) *Bronenosets Potemkin*

1 This account is based on the following sources: material kept in the Eisenstein papers at the Russian State Archive for Literature and the Arts [RGALI], *fond* 1923; I. Rostovtsev, *Bronenosets Potemkin*, Moscow, 1962; N. Kleiman & K. Levina (eds), *Bronenosets Potemkin* [hereafter K & L], Moscow, 1969, a rather unreliable English translation of which appeared as: H. Marshall (ed.), *The Battleship Potemkin. The Greatest Film Ever Made*, New York, 1978; R. Iurenev, *Sergei Eizenshtein. Zamysli. Fil my. Metod. Chast pervaia: 1898–1929*, Moscow, 1985; O. Bulgakowa, *Sergej Eisenstein. Eine Biographie*, Berlin 1997. Specific references are given only to other sources, to direct quotations, or to original or controversial material cited from the above.
2 The relevant minutes are reproduced in: K & L, p. 24; Marshall, pp. 453–4.
3 *ESW4*, p. 446.
4 Shutko was an Old Bolshevik who had once studied theatre and worked with Meyerhold in 1904, later joining the Bolshevik underground. As adviser on *The Strike*, he had acted as Eisenstein's protector, patron and friend.
5 The correspondence has been translated in: J. Leyda (ed.), *Eisenstein 2. A Premature Celebration of Eisenstein s Centenary*, Calcutta 1985, pp. 1–8.
6 *ESW4*, pp. 143–52.
7 Letter dated 5 July 1928; RGALI, 1923/1/68.

8   The minutes of this meeting are in: K & L, p. 25–6; Marshall, pp. 56–7.
9   *ESW4*, p. 169.
10 Interview with Eisenstein, *Vecherniaia Moskva*, 28 July 1925, reprinted in: K & L, p. 54. This is one of several interesting documents not included in Marshall.
11 Rostovtsev, pp. 72–3.
12 *The Nibelungs* [Die Nibelungen, dir. Fritz Lang, 2 parts, 1924]; *Kinogazeta*, 7 July 1925, cited in: Iurenev, pp. 109–10.
13 Strauch's recollection in: K & L, pp. 59–60.
14 K & L, p. 61.
15 *ESW4*, pp. 169–71.
16 Letter dated 14 October 1925; K & L, p. 79.
17 Curiously *The Highest Wave* also featured a revolutionary sailor who took refuge in Romania.
18 *Izvestiia* (Odessa edn), 13 September 1925, cited in: K & L, p. 65.
19 Bulgakowa, p. 78.
20 Reviews appeared in *Pravda*, 16 February 1923, and *Izvestiia*, 17 February 1923.
21 Liovshin's reminiscences 40 years later are included in: K & L, pp. 71–6; Marshall, pp. 63–7.
22 *ESW4*, p. 167.
23 Iurenev, p. 123.
24 *ESW4*, p. 158.
25 The Red Navy was put at the film-makers' disposal on the personal orders of the People's Commissar for the Army and the Navy, Mikhail Frunze.
26 *ESW4*, p. 157.
27 *ESW4*, p. 168.
28 *ESW4*, pp. 168–9.
29 *ESW4*, p. 158.
30 Part of Nuné's unused script was utilized for another anniversary film, devoted to the armed workers' uprising in Moscow in 1905, *Krasnaia Presnia*, directed by Abram Room, Leo Mur and others and released on 19 February 1926, exactly a month after *Potemkin*; K & L, p. 56.
31 K. Shutko, '1905–1917–1925', *Kinozhurnal ARK*, November/December 1925, p. 4; K & L, p. 54.
32 Alexandrov's recollections in: K & L, p. 81.
33 *ESW4*, pp. 181–2.
34 Iurenev, p. 144.

2. Analysis

Since there is no definitive version of *The Battleship Potemkin* I have followed the version held in the BFI National Film Archive. Because there is already a published shot-by-shot description by David Mayer I have avoided a detailed repetition and referred to particular shots in Mayer's account where this seemed particularly helpful. I hope that this analysis is sufficiently detailed to be useful and sufficiently general to apply to most versions of the film in distribution.

The five parts of *The Battleship Potemkin* follow the five-act structure of classical theatrical drama. Nevertheless Eisenstein confided to his diary on 30 July 1934:

> The paradox of *Potemkin* lies in the fact that the successive stages in the epic development of events appear at the same time as elements in the correct sequence of actions according to the classical model of tragedy: more precisely, in the fact that they were taken and heard from the events *as they happened*. It is a mistake to think that history is like this, or that 'history is inherently dramatic'. History is always dramatic, but in this case there is an enormous shift in our attitude towards history and it is only for this reason that the epic appeared simultaneously to be a 'classical tragedy'.[1]

Eisenstein deployed this classical structure to produce what has become a classic, if not *the* classic example of revolutionary cinema. The five parts in the epic are:

Part 1: Men and Maggots
Part 2: Drama on the Quarterdeck
Part 3: An Appeal from the Dead
Part 4: The Odessa Steps
Part 5: Meeting the Squadron.

Each part of the film moves from passive to active mood. In Part 1 the prevailing atmosphere of quiet endurance moves to active resistance to the rotten meat; in Part 2 the change is from submissiveness and acquiescence in the proposed execution to mutiny; in Part 3 from mourning for the dead sailor to anger and mobilization; Part 4 develops from peaceful demonstrations of solidarity between towns-people and crewmen, through the massacre on the Odessa Steps to the battleship firing its guns in anger on the military headquarters; the concluding part of the film moves from uncertainty and insecurity over the approaching fleet's reaction to triumph and the flight to safety as the battleship sails through the fleet to the accompaniment of cheers. This structure ensures that each part of the film contains within it the tensions involved in the dialectical clash between thesis and antithesis, which is resolved in a concluding synthesis that progresses the action to its next stage.

Although the Odessa Steps sequence is the most famous part of *Potemkin*, and constitutes its emotional and ideological heart, it comes towards the end, rather than at the temporal centre, of the film. But it does not come at the very end of the film: emotional tragedy is followed by apparent emotional triumph. This account will broadly follow the chronology of the completed work and concludes with some thematic points for further consideration.

Part 1: Men and Maggots

The Russian title for the first part of the film is 'Liudi i chervi': as David Bordwell has pointed out, this literally means 'men and worms'.[2] The Russian word for a maggot of this type is *lichinka* and Eisenstein's intention here was to suggest a metaphor: on the one hand, men (sailors) and the worms in the meat they are given to eat; on the other, men (officers) and the worms (sailors) who have to serve under them and are treated as less than human. This echoes the distinction made in Dostoyevsky's *Crime and Punishment*, where Raskolnikov tries to make a similar distinction between men and lice (*chelovek i voshch*). Hence the underlying class antagonism that is soon made visually obvious is made clear in the opening titles.

The Battleship Potemkin opens with five alternating establishing shots of waves crashing against first rocks then a jetty: a storm is brewing. These shots may also be read as a dramatic statement of the superior capabilities of cinema over the theatre that Eisenstein had so recently abandoned: no stage production could begin with waves crashing against rocks, except perhaps on film, or through suggestive sound effects. One contemporary critic observed:

> At the beginning of the film we see the beating of the waves, and the rhythm of the sea then develops in the following frames, concealing with growing strength the energy that is contained in the beating and movement of the waves. In theatre this would be impossible.[3]

The first intertitle, citing Lenin, associates the brewing storm with the coming revolution: 'Revolution is the only lawful, equal, effectual war. It was in Russia that this war was declared and begun.'[4] In the original version of the film the opening quotation was from Trotsky, but this was subsequently altered for political reasons, as Trotsky was already out of favour with Stalin and was expelled from the Party in 1927 and sent into internal exile in 1928. From this symbol of the universal and the eternal we cut to a specific shot of two battleships, one seen from the deck of the other, and then to two sailors on the battleship, later identified as the 'Potemkin'.[5] These sailors are two of only five named characters in the film, and we have been introduced to them less than one minute into the action. They are: Vakulinchuk, who is to sacrifice his life for the revolutionary struggle, and Matiushenko, who will lead the mutinous vessel to escape across the Black Sea to Romania in the final sequence of the film. Significantly the names of the two sailors are obviously Ukrainian, whereas the three officers named later are equally obviously Russian: the class difference is here underlined by an implied colonial relationship between the two Slav neighbours. The two sailors engage in an animated discussion, waving their arms about to emphasize their strength of feeling: 'We, the sailors of the Potemkin, must stand in the first lines of the revolution with our brothers, the workers.'

The camera cuts to a distinctly unconvincing shot of a model ship bobbing about on the water and the next title introduces a sequence of 16 contrasting-angled shots of the off-duty watch. Bare-chested men in hammocks are shown sleeping in a series of distinctly homoerotic frames: we shall return to this apparent subtext later. The boatswain, in a dark uniform that contrasts with the light reflecting off the bare backs and chests of the sleeping sailors, enters, moving among them awkwardly, suspiciously searching for something to report. The title remarks that he is 'Vigilant but clumsy' and he gets caught up in the lines of the hammocks, lashing out with a rope and needlessly hitting the bare back of a young sleeping sailor, who bursts into tears at the pointlessness of this attack. He is in turn comforted by another crewman and recovers his composure.

A title introduces us to Vakulinchuk again, this time bare-chested, gesticulating emphatically and reading from a paper in his hands: 'Comrades, the time has come to act.' Four shots with alternating angles intercut Vakulinchuk with the sailors in their hammocks waking up and nodding assent to his call: 'What are we waiting for? All Russia is rising. Are we to be the last?' The next seven shots establish the sailors' growing agreement.

We cut to the title 'Morning'. On the upper deck an indolent-looking officer in a dark jacket and with his hands nonchalantly placed in the pockets of his white trousers, smirks as he looks down in a series of shots on the sailors gathering on the two lower decks, inspecting the carcasses of meat that will constitute their rations and complaining among themselves. There is a play of light and shade and the spatial relationships between upper and lower decks reflect and reinforce the social relationships between officers and sailors. The deck officer, his face like a hawk (an example of Eisenstein's use of typage as exemplified in his first feature film *The Strike*), also looks down on the crew: Vakulinchuk appears behind him, but retreats. The time for action has not yet come, but this is a clear intimation that the established order is about to be challenged.

Titles intercut with shots of the carcass express the men's concern: 'We've had enough garbage to eat!' and 'A dog wouldn't eat this.' The ship's doctor, Smirnov, is identified in a title: he argues with Vakulinchuk, who demands 'Throw it overboard!' Smirnov removes his pince-nez (a sure sign of a member of the bourgeoisie), folds them double and examines the meat. The maggots are clearly seen through the magnification of the pince-nez: it is only through them that he can physically see the maggots (worms) in the meat and yet, despite this, he still refuses to recognize (intellectually see) their existence. Smirnov speaks: 'These are not maggots ... Merely dead fly eggs that will wash off in salt water.' He contemptuously holds the tail of the carcass up in Vakulinchuk's face. He brushes it away: 'The Japanese feed Russian prisoners better than we're fed.' In other words, the tsarist empire's enemy in the Russo-Japanese War feeds its prisoners better than the empire sees fit to feed the armed forces that are defending it. The next

6. (a. & b.) Sailors black and white

title repeats Vakulinchuk's earlier remark 'We've had enough garbage!' Smirnov and the deck officer leave, still arguing with the dissatisfied sailors. Smirnov turns and addresses the men in what he intends to be a final dismissive gesture: 'The meat is good. No further discussion.' This tyrannical attitude exacerbates the dissatisfaction and the two officers indignantly turn their backs, leaving the officer identified as Senior Officer Giliarovsky to disperse the malcontents.

A cook inspects the controversial carcass, sniffs it, looks around to see if he is being observed, sniffs it again and carries it into the mess kitchen, where he starts to hack at it with an axe. Two sailors enter and try to persuade him to stop preparing the meat. Close-ups of the meat are interspersed with shots of the axe and the sailors arguing.

The argument is left unresolved and the film cuts to the barrel of a cannon. A sailor sits astride the cannon pushing a swab brush, dripping with oil, into the barrel in a rhythmic motion which some have argued has sexual connotations. Clearly the cannon may easily be interpreted as a phallic symbol, but it is here being 'penetrated' by the swab cloth, which would mean that the sexual imagery in this particular sequence was, to say the least, unconventional. This particular image is intercut with shots of other cleaning activities on board the ship. This frenetic activity demonstrates the discipline and solidarity of the men and perhaps also represents a form of sublimation.

The sequence ends with a cut to a giant cauldron of boiling soup being stirred with a ladle. This literal image of the preparation of the sailors' food also doubles as a metaphor for the trouble that is brewing on board, for which the very same food is but a catalyst. The mess tables are lowered from the ceiling from which they are suspended, swinging from side to side with the motion of the battleship. This swinging motion heightens the sense of uncertainty and tension. A petty officer inspects the mess and barks out his orders. The metal bowls from which the sailors are expected to eat their soup are laid out. These images are intercut with repeated shots of the soup boiling in the cauldron as the tension builds to a climax. Viewed from below through a steel grating, three sailors are seen talking. On deck others talk animatedly while eating bread and dried fish, spreading salt on the bread and drinking water. The poverty of their diet is thus emphasized and the next title tells us: 'The anger of the sailors overflowed bounds.'

From a shot of two sailors sharing their mug of water the film cuts to Giliarovsky descending the stairs to inspect the mess. We thus see him from the sailors' point of view. He is met with sullen resentment. He inspects a screened locker, checks its contents and turns to look at the mess tables: their swinging motion momentarily mesmerizes and amuses him. There is a cut to the last title in the English-language version of this part of *The Battleship Potemkin*: 'The Canteen': this is the onboard store from which the sailors purchase their extra rations and we see them passing money through an open porthole and receiving their canned goods in return. One sailor looks around uneasily and freezes in position as he sees Giliarovsky approaching. There is a moment of tension but the officer moves on. He meets the deck officer with the hawk-like face. In the Russian version of *Potemkin* there is a title at this point: 'The sailors have refused to eat the soup.' This title is not in the English-language version, but it helps to explain why the two officers go below deck to the mess and exchange words. The deck officer starts back up the stairs, giving Giliarovsky instructions that merely leave him confused: he shrugs his shoulders and leaves as well.

Once again we see from below and through a grille sailors talking on deck: the patterns of light and shade emphasize the emerging mood of conflict and confrontation. The deck officer comes to see the cook: the spotted light patterns of the grille on the cook's face emphasize his lowly position in relation to the officer. The cook opens the door to the mess kitchen where the soup is still boiling away in the cauldrons. Another cook emerges to report to the deck officer: his face is patterned by the shadow of the grille. The scene cuts to three sailors washing and drying the china dishes used for the officers' meals: the sailor washing the dishes is the man on the receiving end of the boatswain's lash in the sleeping quarters earlier. The horizontal stripes on his tee-shirt contrast with the white uniforms of the other two and the vertical strips of wood covering the wall behind them. Once more this device is used to heighten the increasing sense of conflict and confrontation. The china crockery and (presumably silver) cutlery for the officers contrast with the metal dishes for the sailors that we saw in the earlier scenes of the mess.

The sailor doing the washing suddenly notices an inscription round the rim of one of the plates. It is a quotation from the Lord's Prayer: 'Give us this day our daily bread.'[6] As he turns the plate to read the inscription, so a moving title spells it out. Slowly the implications of the quotation dawn on the sailor as we see his face in close-up. He angrily discusses its significance with the other two sailors as his face distorts with rage. He swings his arm round like a discus thrower and smashes the plate on the corner of the table, sending the cutlery flying in all directions. The image fades to the title introducing the second part of the film.

Part 2: Drama on the Quarterdeck

The Russian title for the second part of *Potemkin* is 'drama na Tendre', which has been variously translated as 'drama on the quarterdeck', 'drama at Tendra' and 'drama in Tendre Harbour'.[7] The English title has 'Drama on the Quarterdeck' because, even though the original Russian title accurately describes the mooring place of the ship in the inlet at Tendra, it is precisely on the quarterdeck that this particular drama actually unfolds. The fact that in naval tradition the quarterdeck has been largely reserved for officers gives the location of the action in this part of the film a particular poignancy.

Part 2 begins with a side shot of a bugler giving the signal for the crew to assemble on the quarterdeck. This is followed by a 45-degree angle shot and then a repetition of the first shot, but this time in close-up. The deck is empty apart from three officers: the St Andrew's ensign, the emblem of the tsarist navy, flutters on the stern of the battle-ship. The sailors rush forward in response to the bugle call and line up on both sides of the deck. A shot from above makes the sailors appear to frame the cannons, the officers and the ensign. This sequence ends with a closer shot of the officers.

A title announces 'Captain Golikov' and he emerges from below deck, straightening his tie and followed by Giliarovsky. There is a montage of contrasting shots of Golikov, the officers, the sailors, the quarterdeck: this serves to set up the framework of the growing tension. Golikov speaks, intercut with titles, 'Those satisfied with the food...' '... two steps forward.' The captain points peremptorily with his left hand and the officers and a few sailors step forward as an automatic reaction to his command. Golikov is visibly shaken that the whole crew has not acted in a similarly automatic reaction. The film cuts to an officer nervously fiddling with his strap, and then to the recalcitrant sailors, as the tension mounts. The next title is more emphatic: 'Forward!', delivered this time as an order. The officer continues to play with his strap while Golikov fumes, threatening, 'All the others will hang from the yard-arm!'

As the threat is uttered, Golikov points upwards towards the yard-arm. There is a cut to the yard-arm, silhouetted against the sky like a crucifix. An officer smirks. Three sailors look up in fear; then three others; then an older sailor with a visible shell scar on his forehead. There is a further cut to the mast, where the older sailor imagines the spectre of corpses hanging from the upper and lower yard-arm as punishment. Then two officers are seen smiling with satisfaction at Golikov's firm hand. But the captain is restless and gives another order: 'Call the marines!'

The film cuts to Golikov, then to the quarterdeck as a whole. Another title tells us: 'Under the pretext of leaving the ranks Matiushenko rallies the men to the gun-turret.' We see the sailors on both sides of the deck arguing about what they should do next, contrasted with the officers in the middle. The title 'To the turret' is intercut with shots of the sailors. In long shot we see the marines marching in: they line up beneath the gun-turret. There is a cut to Matiushenko, then the title 'Men...!', a cut to the sailors, and then another title 'Now!' The drama on the quarterdeck is now reaching its first climax: the sailors leave their orderly lines and assemble beneath the gun-turret. The success of Matiushenko's call is underlined by the next title: 'Most of the sailors reached the turret.' One last group runs across the quarterdeck to join the others under the turret and behind the assembled marines.

There is a cut to the officers, and to Giliarovsky in particular. The turmoil among the sailors contrasts with the steeliness of Giliarovsky: 'Stop! Back to your ranks!' Around twenty sailors who remain on the quarterdeck are forced by the officers back to the edge of the deck. Some try to escape through the captain's hatchway and he notices. A close up of Captain Golikov is followed by the title 'Get away from there, you rascals!' The tone of his order contrasts with Matiushenko's earlier fraternal appeal. The captain angrily shakes his fist, pulls the sailors back from 'his' hatchway and roughly pushes them to the ground. He snarls, 'I'll kill you like dogs!', continuing the man v. animals imagery of 'men and maggots/worms'.

There is concern among the ranks as Golikov orders the marines to their firing position. In another close-up he gives the order: 'Cover them with a tarpaulin.' The officers obey, and confirm their obedience by saluting him. We then see a close-up of Giliarovsky grinning and twirling his moustache: he is clearly enjoying the captain's forceful action. There is a diagonal shot of the quarterdeck with the cannons and shadow falling from bottom left to top right. The officers bring in a rolled-up tarpaulin. One marine looks round and watches the officers as they unroll the tarpaulin: this shot expresses the marine's doubts. These are reinforced by a shot of the quarterdeck with the cannon on the right-hand side like an erect phallus, while the sailors swarm beneath the cannons and behind the marines. Through this sexual imagery the strength of the (literally) rising tension, and in particular the rising opposition to traditional authority, are emphasized.

The next title repeats the order: 'Cover them!' The officers unroll the tarpaulin while the sailors who have been trapped on the deck cower by the railings. The tarpaulin is thrown over them like a funeral shroud, while the marines look impassively on. There follows an ironic waist-down shot of the white trousers of two officers retreating from the tarpaulin. The next title is 'Attention!' In a series of rapid cuts we are shown the officers' faces, the cannons, the quarterdeck with the tarpaulin covering the trapped sailors top left, the officers top and bottom right, the marines and guns across the middle, the mass of the sailors who have successfully responded to Vakulinchuk's call bottom right. The marines step forward and Giliarovsky steps on to the captain's rostrum. There is then a rather obvious studio reconstruction shot of the gun-turret, front on (which was later used in one of the Russian advertisements for the film) and then a shot of a model of the battleship, aptly described by Mayer as 'seemingly suspended between the glassy water and the still sky'.[8] This suspense shot was filmed in the Sandunov Baths in central Moscow. As Eisenstein recalled in his memoirs:

Try filming a mutiny in those conditions!
But Russians can overcome any obstacle and the mutiny was filmed!
True, there is a side view of the battleship in the picture ... but this was taken in the Moorish halls of the Sandunov Baths in Moscow, the grey hull of a model battleship rocking in the water.[9]

An Orthodox priest appears at the top of the stairs and raises his ornate cross: 'Lord, reveal Thyself to the unruly.' The priest's appearance at this critical juncture in the drama on the quarterdeck underlines the complicity of Russian Christianity in the tsarist autocracy, in which the Orthodox Church was run, as it had been since the time of Peter the Great, as a department of state called the Holy Synod. But the story that the priest was played by Eisenstein himself is apocryphal: the role was in fact played by an unknown man chosen simply because

he represented the archetype of an old Russian priest, another prime
example of Eisenstein's principle of 'typage'. The story acquired
currency because there is in existence a photograph of the director
dressed up as the priest in order to show the 'type' playing the role
what to do and how to do it (see p. 26). The priest's prayer is followed

7. (a, b & c) Drama on the quarterdeck. The old order [thesis]; the tarpaulin episode [antithesis]; the new order [synthesis]

by movement under the tarpaulin. The priest's head is seen in close-up: he is silhouetted against steam, shot so that it suggests a stormy sky and a return to the storm analogy in the opening shots of the film. Giliarovsky is then also seen in close-up.

The next title gives the fatal order, which comes from Giliarovsky rather than the captain: 'At the tarpaulin – Fire!' The marines raise their rifles and there is a montage of different shots: Vakulinchuk; the sailors around him stepping back; the movement under the tarpaulin of the trapped sailors; the marines again; the officers. Tension increases as the priest taps the ornate cross that we have already seen to mark the passage of time and an officer fiddles nervously with his sword. Once more the montage links the church and the armed forces as twin pillars of the autocracy. The confrontation is approaching its climax. Beneath the tarpaulin the sailors fall to their knees, presumably in a gesture begging for mercy, while the marines take aim. Another rapid montage sequence pits Vakulinchuk raising his head against the rifles; the priest's cross marking time; a lifebelt showing the ship's name; the double-headed eagle – symbol of tsarist autocracy – on the ship's prow; a bugle held at ease; the tarpaulin. It is clear that Vakulinchuk has decided that the moment for decisive action has arrived: 'Vakulinchuk decides.' A close-up shows Giliarovsky smiling as he gives his next order; 'Fire!', then Vakulinchuk cries out, 'Brothers!' Then he asks the marines, 'Do you realize who you are shooting?' We see a close-up of a Central Asian marine: 'The Marines faltered.' Some rifles are lowered: Giliarovsky shouts and gesticulates angrily, outlined against a background of sea and sky, the natural elements against which his struggle is hopeless. With increasing desperation Giliarovsky repeats his order twice as the marines lower their rifles, and then he runs forward to face them, standing in the firing line: 'SHOOT, damn you!' A close-up shows Giliarovsky's desperation, as the marines all lower their rifles. He shouts hysterically, and runs forward to disarm one marine. The collapse of his authority is now complete.

Taking Giliarovsky's place literally as well as metaphorically, Vakulinchuk gives his own order to the sailors: 'To the rifles, brothers!' The use of the term 'brothers' underlines that his is a different, egalitarian rather than hierarchical, relationship with the crew. He climbs on to the phallic gun-turret and shouts, 'Kill the brutes!' and then simply, 'Kill them!' Here there is a neat antithesis to the earlier remark by Captain Golikov: when he shouts 'I'll kill you like dogs!' he does so in a context

8. *Eisenstein* donning the priest's garb

that emphasizes his callous cruelty against the sailors as 'innocents', whereas when Vakulinchuk calls the officers 'brutes' he does so at a moment when the audience has just been presented with unambiguous evidence of their brutality. Furthermore the Russian word used is *drakon* or 'dragon', a mythical beast, which clearly implies that the authority and power of the officer class are themselves based on mythology rather than justice. This is reinforced by the fact that St George is also a Russian saint and the tale of his slaying of the evil tyranny of the dragon would resonate with Russian audiences. Vakulinchuk, in this reading, is St George. Perhaps as a reminder, or rather as the embodiment, of the officers' cruelty, Vakulinchuk's 'Kill them!' is immediately followed by a shot of the arch-'dragon' Giliarovsky.

In response to Vakulinchuk's call the previously cornered sailors throw off their tarpaulin and join their comrades, fighting with the officers to take control of the ship. We see a close-up of the St Andrew's ensign, flying from the stern. The officers try to escape down the captain's hatchway from which the sailors were earlier diverted by the captain. Meanwhile the sailors take rifles from the stores. Giliarovsky, now running very scared indeed, tries to escape: the tables have been turned and he is manhandled by the sailors whom he has previously himself abused. The officers and sailors brawl, symbolically trampling the tarpaulin that so recently threatened to provide a funeral shroud. Rifles are passed through a porthole in a visual echo of the earlier sequence involving the rations. An officer is wrapped in the tarpaulin, once more underlining the change in fortunes and the overturning of established patterns of authority.

But the victory of the mutineers is far from complete or secure. Giliarovsky, now armed, pursues Vakulinchuk. The priest raises his cross in a now redundant gesture threatening excommunication and warns the men, 'You are fighting God.' Yet again the Orthodox Church is identified with the *ancien régime*. Amidst the fighting on the quarterdeck the priest waves his cross specifically at Vakulinchuk and calls, 'Away with you, Chaldean!'[10] In response, Vakulinchuk tries to throttle the priest but Giliarovsky intervenes. Meanwhile an officer is dragged along the deck by the sailors. Shots of Giliarovsky and Vakulinchuk in hand-to-hand combat are intercut in another montage sequence with shots of the general mêlée on the quarterdeck. The priest's cross falls to the deck and sticks into it like an axe. He falls backwards down the stairs. The church militant has been disposed of, but Giliarovsky and Vakulinchuk are still locked in mortal combat.

In the officers' quarters an officer, panic-stricken, tramples on the piano (as others have just trampled on the tarpaulin) and shoots a sailor to save his own skin. Other sailors enter and throw him to the ground. Outside an officer clambers on to the gun-turret. There is firing inside and out. An officer is thrown overboard. We see the gun-turret from the side: a sailor knocks an officer into the sea, where he is visible under water. Dr Smirnov, who had given the rotten meat a clean bill of health, is captured and held upside-down as he clings to a rope. He is dragged up some steps. The priest, who has previously fallen down those steps, opens one eye to survey the scene. As the fighting is continuing, he closes it again, waiting, like Shakespeare's Falstaff, until it is safe for him to make his getaway. Smirnov is manhandled and thrown into the sea: 'Down to feed the maggots.' His pince-nez are left hanging from a rope on the ship's side, an ironic reminder of his blindness to reality. Victory is still not quite complete as fighting continues on the quarterdeck and the sailors swarm the gun-turret. Then there is cause for celebration: 'Brothers! We've won!'

The officers' quarters are empty: we see the trampled piano with sheet music on which the name of Tchaikovsky is clearly visible. This reminds us that the culture and civilization of the officer class is only a veneer: when cornered, the veneer dissolves and the class shows itself in its true, repressive and brutal colours. Just as the officer previously cornered in the officers' quarters had shot a sailor to save his own skin, so too he trampled on the piano and on the music of one of Russia's greatest composers to the same end. Given what Giliarovsky is about to do to Vakulinchuk, this reminder is a timely one.

The film cuts from the officers' quarters to the gun-turret, the scene of the sailors' triumph. The title: 'The brutal Giliarovsky is after Vakulinchuk' is followed by shots of the chase across the ship. The Russian title describes Giliarovsky as *ozverelyi* which translates as 'brutalized' or 'made beastly', repeating the man/animal imagery from the first part of the film. Giliarovsky's dark jacket contrasts once more with Vakulinchuk's white uniform, his slyness and concealment with the sailor's openness and vulnerability. Giliarovsky takes aim and, like a true coward, shoots Vakulinchuk in the back of the head. The wounded sailor falls overboard and his body is caught by a rope. If Smirnov's pince-nez are the thesis, Vakulinchuk's dying body is the antithesis from which the synthesis of the mutiny will emerge: the triumph is turning into tragedy. The celebrations on the quarterdeck are intercut with shots of Vakulinchuk's suspended body. He struggles and slips. As he does so another sailor notices what is happening: 'Vakulinchuk is overboard!' The sailors clamber out: 'Save Vakulinchuk!' They dive into the sea and swim towards their dying comrade, still suspended just above the surface of the waters. Then Vakulinchuk slips into the sea and the sailors carry his blood-stained corpse, as it obviously now is, on board the ship. The next title points up the irony, 'And he, who first raised the cry of revolt, was the first to fall at the hand of the executioner.'

A launch enters the frame at bottom right and steams diagonally upwards to top left across the screen. A guard of honour lines the deck; sailors stand to attention at the prow and around the shrouded corpse, while a black standard flutters from the flagstaff at the stern. 'Vakulinchuk's body is being ferried: To the shore.' In soft focus we see the lighthouse at the end of the jetty marking the seaward side of the harbour. The title tells us simply: 'Odessa'. The launch crosses the screen left to right, then right to left, against the light of the setting sun. The next title locates us more precisely: 'A tent on the new pier of Odessa was the last shelter of Vakulinchuk.' This is followed by a series of *contre-jour* shots of sailing boats and a rowing boat in the harbour. We see in medium close-up the candles on Vakulinchuk's body and the simple hand-written note 'For a spoonful of soup', an echo of the biblical quotation seen earlier, 'Give us this day our daily bread.' The protest against the inhumanity of man to man has resulted in one further act of brutal inhumanity, one more senseless loss of life. The camera cuts from the candle to Vakulinchuk's face, to his feet, and then to the opening of the tent, framing a shot of the sailing boats in the harbour. Part 2 concludes with a series of elegiac shots of sailing boats moving slowly across the screen against a background of the setting sun. A small dog trots past the tent opening and a large vessel gradually blocks out the failing light and the scene fades into Part 3.

Part Two has taken us from the bugler's summons to the quarter-deck, through the disciplinary confrontation over sailors' attitude towards the rotten meat, to mutiny and death, which will now provide the catalyst for a broader disaffection with tsarist autocracy. The seeds of a more general revolt have now been sown.

Part 3: An Appeal from the Dead

The third part of *The Battleship Potemkin* begins with a long shot of the port. A title tells us that it is night. This is followed by a sequence of shots: masts and derricks in the port; ships docked by the jetty; morning mists; the sea; and then travelling shots of other ships. Dawn is breaking, the images are painterly and the mood elegiac.

Once again we see the view from inside the tent where Vakulinch-uk's body lies, and then the outside, draped with black cloth. A general view of the harbour shows a man fishing in the middle distance: life goes on and dawn is breaking. A large vessel is moored by the jetty. The next title tells us: 'The quay aroused curiosity.' A man approaches the tent as a second fisherman sets up his tackle on the quayside. Two black-shawled women cross the front of the frame from right to left. Their curiosity aroused, they approach somewhat tentatively as two men approach symmetrically from the left. From inside the tent looking out we see a crowd gathering. The camera cuts to Vakulinch-uk's head and shoulders and then to an old peasant woman who kneels to trim the wick of the candle that has gone out overnight. The imagery is unmistakably religious. A medium shot of the two anglers shows them waiting patiently for something to happen: even the cat between them barely stirs. A close-up of the rekindled candle in Vakulinchuk's hands fills the screen, followed by the hand-written slogan, 'For a spoonful of soup'. All the while the crowd is growing larger. The men remove their caps as a sign of respect. Even two obviously bourgeois ladies with elaborate lace-decorated parasols appear. The sails of a ship are lowered as if in a parallel gesture of respect. A title remarks, 'Along with the sun, rose the whole city!'

In the next shot the screen is divided into three vertical panels: the two side panels are black and the middle one shows a narrow flight of steps, as if viewed from between a narrow gateway. A sudden dissolve shows the steps thronged with people descending purposefully towards the harbour. A title: 'The battleship at anchorage' seems at first somewhat out of place, but the intertitles in this sequence of shots are intended to convey the role of fragmented rumour in spreading the message of the mutiny to the citizens of Odessa. Shots of crowds descending steps, crossing bridges and edging along the streets towards the harbour jetty are intercut with a series of titles: '... uprising...', '... the shore...', '... a dead sailor...' Just before this last title we see the crowd crossing the jetty bottom left to top right, viewed from above through the ropes of a ship's mast; the title is followed by an overhead shot of the crowd circling round the tent which is now 'guarded' by three women. A small boy looks at Vakulinchuk's upturned cap and adds another coin to the collection: all generations mourn the dead sailor. Once more we see his head and shoulders and the slogan, repeated like a leitmotif throughout this part of the film. A hand drops two more coins into the cap. In a medium shot of the tent and the surrounding crowd two women with lace parasols cross the foreground from right to left: apart from them, the crowd at this stage is overwhelmingly composed of working-class men, women and children.

A series of carefully choreographed general shots establishes the scale of the crowd that is assembling. First we see the crowd crossing the front of the frame, while many more approach along the breakwater that stretches across the left side and back of the frame into the distance (Mayer's shot 676); then a shot from above (possibly from the masthead of one of the sailing ships) shows the crowd moving across the frame from top right to middle left; next, an overhead shot has the crowd moving downwards from top to bottom middle of the frame; lastly the camera pans upwards tracing the curving course of the breakwater out of the frame towards top right (Mayer's shot 680). These changes of angle and the subsequent intercutting of shots of the breakwater with views of crowds descending steps, crossing bridges, and streaming endlessly into the distance, all emphasize that the crowd is coming from all directions, echoing and illustrating the earlier title 'Along with the sun, rose the whole city.'

An overhead shot of the tent shows the crowd surrounding it in a swirling pattern. A woman in black harangues the crowd: among them is the woman with the white parasol. Everyone is united in grief and anger. The first woman gesticulates as she speaks: 'We will remember' ... 'For a spoonful of soup!' A young sailor also gesticulates as he reads the appeal to the townspeople from the mutinous crew of the battleship 'Potemkin':

People of Odessa!
Before you lies the body of Grigori Vakulinchuk, a sailor cruelly murdered by the senior officer of the battleship 'Potemkin'.
We will avenge ourselves! Death to the oppressors!
The crew of the battleship 'Potemkin'.

The young sailor finishes his appeal. As the ever-growing crowd files past in the background, we see two elderly women grieving, a peasant woman bends low over Vakulinchuk's corpse as if to kiss his face, another elderly woman is seen crying, while an old gentleman removes his pince-nez, overcome with emotion. Not all pince-nez wearers are blind to the tragedy that is unfolding. Two women drop to their knees and bend over to touch the dead man's feet with their heads as a gesture of respect. But there remain those who are unmoved by the occasion, and their indifference only serves to underline the general sense of mourning. One such is a middle-aged moustachioed man wearing a straw hat at a jaunty angle. He puffs his cigarette and smirks in amusement at the scene of mass grief. By contrast the next shot shows the top of a woman's head filling the bottom part of the frame as she kneels at Vakulinchuk's feet. A title calls for 'Eternal memory for the fallen fighters!' A shot of four grieving women gives way to the title 'All for one...', followed by a balancing shot of four men singing: it could be either a lament or a revolutionary song. Their different facial types – the man on the left is distinctly dark-skinned – suggest once again the universality of grief. The next title, '... one...' cuts to a close-up of Vakulinchuk's head and shoulders and back to another title '... for all.'

Another overhead shot shows the whole crowd now gesticulating angrily. Two blind women sing a lament: but this shot is intended to underline once more the universality of grief. A series of group and individual shots confirm this message: we are as individuals alone in our mourning and our sense of loss and yet the common sense of grief acts as a unifying force. Each individual, *pars pro toto*, represents something more than themselves, is part of something greater. Gradually the grief is turning into something else. A student wearing a great-coat shouts to the assembled crowd: 'Down with the executioners!' A series of rapid shots intercuts back views of men's heads as they listen to this message, close-ups of a fist being clenched, men and women in the crowd shouting and gesticulating. The message is getting across. The woman orator in black seen earlier continues to address the crowd. The old woman we have previously seen in tears tosses away her handkerchief and mouths agreement with the orator's call. The men wave their clenched fists, and then the women do likewise. There is unity between the sexes as well as between the generations and the different social classes. The old woman shouts: she is becoming an active rebel, no longer a long-suffering bystander. The crowd responds to the orator, once again with one exception.

A well-dressed but rather bloated middle-aged man stands sneering contemptuously with his thumbs in his waistcoat. The women in the crowd wave their hands in support of the woman in black as she calls on them: 'Mothers and brothers! Let there be no difference or enmity between us!' Close-ups show the well-dressed man smiling, the woman orator, and the man again. He shouts out 'Down with the Jews!'

The original Russian formulation is much stronger than the conventional English translation: the full force of '*Bei zhidov!*' is 'Kill the Yids!' The significance of this remark in the Odessa of 1905 requires some historical explanation. Over the years official attempts had been made to confine the Jewish population of the Russian Empire to the so-called 'Pale of Settlement' (*zona osedlosti*), which included western Poland, Belorussia, and parts of the Ukraine stretching down to Odessa. Following a series of anti-Semitic pogroms in 1881, which resulted in large-scale atrocities, the government renewed its efforts to concentrate the Jewish population of the Empire in the Pale. One consequence of this was an enormous flowering of Jewish cultural activity, centred on Odessa and exemplified by the work of the writer Isaak Babel, who was to collaborate with Eisenstein on a number of unfinished projects. By 1905 Odessa was a multiracial and multicultural city port, and thus also an obvious focus for the activities of extreme right-wing nationalist gangs, known as the 'Black Hundreds' (*chernosotentsy*) who in the years 1905–9 were to terrorize tens of thousands of Jewish victims in an organized series of pogroms. Jewish intellectuals in the Pale of Settlement grouped themselves together into a number of political organizations, one of which, the Jewish Bund, became part of the revolutionary movement led by Lenin's Bolsheviks. Their historical role in the development of Russian socialism was therefore of considerable significance and the anti-Semitic *agent provocateur* depicted here represented a real and dangerous political phenomenon, rather than a mere empty propagandist caricature.

Another close-up of the well-dressed man's smirking face is immediately followed by a close-up of a seaman's furious face as he turns towards the camera and, by clear implication, towards the *agent provocateur*. Others too turn to stare menacingly at him. At first he is oblivious to having made the wrong remark in the wrong place at the wrong time and smiles in self-satisfaction. The sailor, his face contorted with rage, argues with him. The well-dressed man, shocked at the strength of the hostile reaction, pulls his hat down over his face and turns up his collar: this is partly an attempt at concealment, partly an act of self-defence. He tries to leave but is surrounded. His hat is removed as the crowd closes in and he is manhandled and beaten up, disappearing into the angry throng. This whole sequence repeats the swirling action of the sailors on the quarterdeck as they captured the battleship from their officers. Once more the traditional hegemonies are overthrown.

The student harangues the crowd, which is visibly moved. Scenes of the orator are intercut with those of the crowd's reactions. One peasant woman tears off her shawl and twirls it around her head. The next title emphasizes the growing solidarity of the townspeople of Odessa: 'Shoulder to shoulder'. Earlier shots of the crowds advancing towards the harbour are repeated and intercut with titles reflecting revolutionary slogans: 'The land – for us!'; 'Tomorrow – for us!' Still the crowd comes, and the student continues his appeal. A sea of waving fists confirms the effectiveness of his words and a young man tears off his shirt. In response to the agitation a sea of raised fists fills the screen.

The film cuts back, for the first time in Part 3, to the battleship itself. The quarterdeck is seen from above, bisected by the two cannons on the gun-turret. The sailors swarm forward, covering the deck where the confrontation between officers and men took place in Part 2. It is now unequivocally *their* space. We see a head-on shot, followed by a side shot, of the gun-turret, and then the bridge. The mutineers swarm over the whole ship. A closer shot focuses on the bridge and a title announces: 'A delegate from the shore'. In medium close-up a civilian appears among the sailors on the bridge and addresses the crew: 'The enemy has been dealt a decisive blow!' This is the first clearly uttered statement of revolutionary solidarity between the townspeople and the mutineers. A rear view from above shows the civilian delegate gesticu- lating as he addresses the sailors below him: 'Together with the rising workers of all Russia. . .' The title is followed by a closer front shot of the civilian speaking and then an overhead shot of the teeming quarter- deck with the sailors looking up at the bridge: 'We will win!' The sailors raise their white caps and cheer, confirming their own solidarity with the people of Odessa. A series of long and side shots shows the scenes of triumphant celebration. Even the crow's nest is crammed with cheering sailors. The newly forged alliance is endorsed by the next title: 'Tensely and vigilantly the shore watched over the "Potemkin".'

The scene of the action returns to the shore. At the foot of a vast staircase leading down to the harbour a huge crowd of Odessa towns- people stand looking anxiously out to sea. They represent a cross- section of society: some are workers, some shade themselves with parasols. There is a closer shot of a well-dressed group of adults and children. On the left of this group we can clearly see the 'schoolmis- tress' (another example of Eisenstein's typage) who is to play such a crucial part in the Odessa Steps sequence that follows. This is the calm before the storm. Back on the 'Potemkin' an overhead shot shows the quarterdeck, then the gun-turret, with sailors looking aloft. From below we see a sailor in the crow's nest: behind him a huge red flag, the flag of revolution, is raised on the masthead. In the original print this flag is reputed to have been hand-tinted red to enhance the dramatic effect. The sailors cheer: back on land the townspeople echo the cheers and waves. The red flag flutters in the breeze. Mutiny on board the battle-ship 'Potemkin' has become generalized into the revolutionary uprising of 1905. The ship is part of the whole, which it symbolizes: this is in embryonic form the metonymic device that Eisenstein called '*pars pro toto* – one for all and all for one.

Part 4: The Odessa Steps

The pivotal Odessa Steps sequence of *The Battleship Potemkin* may well lay claim to being the most famous single sequence of images in the history of world cinema, and especially of silent montage cinema. It also provides a classic example of poetic licence: a filmic creation of a historical event that in itself never happened but that encapsulates in *microcosm* the *macrocosmic* drama of a more general historical process. In this sense the Odessa Steps sequence is a paradigm of *pars pro toto*.

   Part 4 begins with a title: 'That memorable day the city lived one life with the rebellious battleship.' In the foreground we see the masts and furled sails of a large number of sailing boats moored against the wooden jetty. Then sailors clamber aboard and start casting off. The next title comments: 'White-winged boats flew to the 'Potemkin'.' In the next shot a group of townspeople carrying bundles walks along a gangplank towards one of the boats. A billowing white sail fills the screen: as it glides off-frame to the right the rush of other craft is revealed in the background. The townspeople board a boat, carrying their bundles of provisions for the 'Potemkin'. Two shots show a flotilla of small sailing boats moving left to right, then one of them sailing from top left to bottom right. These varying shots suggest a general movement in all directions and universalize the particular.

   The sequence that follows, and that precedes the actual massacre on the Odessa Steps, was analysed by Eisenstein himself in his 1934 article ' "Eh!" On the Purity of Film Language'. It would be redundant to offer an alternative analysis and I therefore reproduce Eisenstein's own:

In order to demonstrate the compositional interdependence of the plastic aspect of the changing shots I have deliberately chosen an example at random rather than from a climactic scene: fourteen consecutive fragments from the scene that precedes the shooting on the Odessa Steps. The scene where the 'good people of Odessa' (as the 'Potemkin' sailors addressed their appeal to the population of Odessa) send skiffs with provisions alongside the mutinous battleship.

The sending of greetings is constructed on a distinct intersection between two subjects:

1 The skiffs speed towards the battleship.
2 The people of Odessa wave.

In the end the two subjects merge.
The composition is basically on two planes: depth and foreground. The subjects dominate alternately, advancing to the foreground and pushing one another into the background.

The composition is constructed: (1) on the plastic interaction between both planes (within the shot), (2) on the change in line and form on each plane from shot to shot (by montage). In the second case the compositional play is formed from the interaction of the plastic impression of the previous shot in collision or interaction with the succeeding one. (Here the analysis is by purely spatial and linear sign. The rhythmic temporal relationship will be examined elsewhere.)

The movement of the composition (see the attached table, p. 37) takes the following course.

I. The skiffs in motion. A smooth movement parallel to a horizontal cross-section of the shot. The whole field of vision is occupied by the first subject. There is a play of small vertical sails.
II. The intensifying movement of the skiffs of the first subject. (The entrance of the second subject facilitates this.) The second subject comes to the fore with strict rhythm of motionless vertical columns. The vertical lines sketch the plastic disposition of the future figures (IV, V, etc.). The interplay of horizontal waves and vertical lines. The skiff subject is pushed into the background. The plastic subject of the arch appears in the bottom half of the shot.

9. Eisenstein's visual analysis of the skiffs sequence

III. The plastic subject of the arch expands into the whole shot. The play revolves around the change in the frame's articulation from vertical lines to the structure of the arch. The vertical subject is maintained in the movement of small-scale people moving away from the camera. The skiff subject is finally pushed into the background.

IV. The plastic subject of the arch finally occupies the foreground. The arch structure moves into the opposite resolution: the contours of a group forming a circle are sketched in (the parasol completes the composition). The same transition to an opposite also occurs within the vertical construction: the backs of the small-scale people moving into the background are replaced by large-scale static figures filmed from the front. The subject of the movement of the skiffs is maintained by reflection in the expression of the eyes and in their movement along the horizontals.

In the foreground a common compositional variation: an even number of people is replaced by an uneven number. Two becomes three. This 'golden rule' in changing the *mise-en-scène* is supported by a tradition that dates back to the Italian *commedia dell arte* (the direction of the glances also intersects). The arch motif is once more straightened out, this time into an opposite curve. Repeating and supporting it, there is a new parallel arch motif in the *background*: a balustrade. The skiff subject in motion. The eye passes over the whole breadth of the shot along the horizontal.

VI. Sections I-V provide the transposition from the skiff subject to that of the onlookers, developed in five montage sections. The interval V–VI produces a sudden transition back from the onlookers to the skiffs. The composition, which strictly follows the content, suddenly turns all the signs back in the opposite direction. The line of the balustrade is brought suddenly to the foreground, and repeated in the line of the boat's gunwale. It is echoed by the line where the boat comes into contact with the surface of the water. The basic compositional articulation is the same but the treatment is the opposite. V is static. VI is sketched out through the dynamic of the boat in motion. The division into 'three' along the vertical is maintained in both shots. The central element is texturally similar (the woman's blouse and the canvas of the sail). The elements at the sides are sharply contrasted: the dark shapes of the men beside the woman and the white spaces beside the sail. The articulations along the vertical are also contrasted: three figures cut off by the bottom of the frame become a vertical sail cut off by the top of the frame. In the *background* a new subject appears: the battleship seen from the side, cut off at the top (a preparation for Section VII).

VII. Another sudden change of subject. The background subject, the battleship, moves forward into the foreground (the thematic jump from V to VI serves as a kind of *Vorschlag*[11] to the jump from VI to VII). The angle is turned through 180: the shot from the battleship towards the sea is the reverse of VI. This time the side of the battleship is in the *foreground* and is cut off by the *bottom* of the frame. In the background is the sail subject, working in verticals.

The vertical of the sailors. The static gun-barrel continues the line of movement of the boat in the preceding section. The side of the ship appears to be an arch becoming a straight line.

VIII. This repeats IV with greater intensity. The horizontal play of the eyes spreads into a vertical of waving hands. The vertical subject moves from the background into the foreground, repeating the thematic transfer of attention to the onlookers.

IX. Two faces closer up. Generally speaking, an unfortunate combination with the preceding section. A shot with three faces should have been inserted between them. A repetition of Section V, for instance, but also with greater intensity.

This would have produced a 2:3:2 structure. Moreover, the repetition of the familiar group IV-V ending with a new IX would have heightened the perception of the last shot. The situation is saved by a slight enlargement of the close-up.

X. Two faces become one. The arm is raised very energetically up and out of the frame. A correct alternation of faces (if we adopt the correction between VIII and IX): 2:3:2:1. The second pair of shots with the correct enlargement of scale *vis-à-vis* the first pair (a proper repetition with qualitative variation). The line of odd numbers varies both in quantity and quality (the dimension of the faces is different, as is their number, while observing the general characteristics of odd numbers).

XI. Another sudden change of subject. A jump that repeats V–VI but with greater intensity. The vertical *thrust* of the previous shot is repeated in the vertical *sail*. But the vertical of this sail scuds past horizontally. A repetition of the subject of VI with greater intensity. And a repetition of the composition of II with the difference that the subject of the horizontal of the skiffs' motion and the vertical of motionless columns is here fused into a single horizontal transposition of the *vertical* sail. The composition repeats the thematic line of the unity and identity between the skiffs and the people on the shore (before we move on to the final theme of merger: the shore and the battleship via the skiffs).

XII. The sail in XI dissolves into a multitude of vertical sails, scudding along horizontally (a repetition of Section I with heightened intensity). The small sails move in the opposite direction from the large sail.

XIII. Having dissolved into small sails, the large sail is once more reassembled, this time not into a sail but into the flag flying over the

'Potemkin'. There is a new quality in this shot because it is both static and mobile, the mast being vertical and motionless while the flag flutters in the breeze. In formal terms Section XII repeats XI. But the change from sail to banner translates the principle of plastic unification into an ideological and thematic unification. This is no longer just a vertical that in plastic terms joins the separate elements of composition: *this is a revolutionary banner uniting the battleship, the skiffs and the shore.*

XIV. From here there is a natural return from the flag to the battleship. XIV repeats VII. Also with heightened intensity.

This section introduces a new compositional group of *interrelationships between the skiffs and the battleship* as distinct from the first group of *skiffs and the shore.* The first group reflected the subject: 'The skiffs are bringing greetings and gifts from the shore to the battleship'. The second group will express the *fraternization between the skiffs and the battleship.*

The mast with the revolutionary flag serves as a compositional watershed and at the same time as the ideological uniting face for both compositional groups. Section VII, repeated by the first shot in the second group in Section XIV, appears as a sort of *Vorschlag* for the second group and as an element linking the two groups together, like a 'patrol' sent out by the latter group to the former. In the second group the same role will be performed by the shots of the waving figures, cut into the scenes of fraternization between the skiffs and the battleship.

You must not think that both the shooting and montage for these sequences were done according to tables calculated *a priori*. Of course not. But the assembly and the interrelationship of these fragments on the cutting table were clearly dictated by the compositional requirements of film form. These requirements dictated the selection of these fragments from all those available. They established the regularity of the alternation between shots. Actually these fragments, if viewed merely from the standpoint of plot and story, could be arranged in any combination. But the compositional movement through them would scarcely prove in that case to be as regular in construction.[12]

Eisenstein concluded this examination: 'We should not complain of the complexity of this analysis. In comparison with analysis of literary and musical form my analysis is still quite obvious and easy.'

Eisenstein's analysis may not appear 'quite obvious and easy' to the general reader but it does challenge the film viewer to examine each shot for its thematic, compositional and eventually also rhythmic content. It also offers us some pointers to the techniques underlying the construction of the montage for *The Battleship Potemkin* as a whole.

The sequence from the first appearance of the skiffs in the harbour of Odessa to the shot of the red flag flying on the mast of the 'Potemkin' represents an idyllic interval between the elegy of the mourning scenes for Vakulinchuk and the consequent agitation, on the one hand, and the violence of the actual Odessa Steps sequence on the other. It constitutes the calm before the brewing storm. It also introduces us to some of the principal characters peopling the Odessa Steps, most notably the woman who is always referred to as the 'schoolmistress' (because, thanks to Eisensteinian typage, she looks like one), the disabled boy and a number of well-dressed women whose presence emphasizes the solidarity between all classes of the city's population and the mutinous crew of the battleship. In the midst of the calm, these characters represent a *Vorschlag* – to use Eisenstein's own term – of the storm that is about to break, a storm whose imminence was indicated by the very opening sequences of the film.

A mother stands on the steps with her little son. She takes the basket he is holding and shows him how to wave at the battleship. A boy and girl are also held aloft to wave. The next shots capture the bottom half of a woman in black with a white parasol and a woman in white with a black parasol. The balance between their vertical figures crosscuts the shadows falling across the steps, recalling the contrast between light and shade, upper and lower deck, in the shots of the battleship before the mutiny and the tension that that contrast represented. The next title says simply: 'Suddenly', and suddenly the atmosphere does change.

A close-up shows a woman's head jerking backwards, her hair falling over her face, and then the women with their parasols and the disabled boy rush forward down the steps. The white parasol fills the screen obscuring what is happening and adding to the sense of sudden disorientation. Then we see the side wall of the steps with figures running forward from left to right down the steps. The legless boy uses his hands to scuttle downwards; he turns round to look back for a second and then continues. An overhead shot shows the statue of the Duc de Richelieu, former governor of the city, at the top of the steps in the foreground with the backs of the escaping citizens beyond it. In the foreground a group of Cossacks, wearing white jackets and black

trousers and boots, appear at the top of the steps. They are carrying rifles with fixed bayonets. Because of the camera angle their presence looms over the whole steps and below the crowd continues its flight.

An angle shot shows another woman in high-heeled shoes (an obvious bourgeois trait) picking herself up from the ground where she has fallen and running forwards, again from left to right. A long shot highlights the disarray of the panic-stricken crowd at the top of the steps as they flee, descending towards the camera. The legs of a man in

10. (a, b & c) The Odessa Steps sequence: the crowd before, during and after

a suit buckle beneath him. Other bodies fall across the screen. A young boy, his path of escape blocked by the bodies, sits on the steps, covers his ears to shut out the sound of gunfire and screams. Different kinds of movements echo the different swirling movements earlier on the quarterdeck. The crowd continues its forward flight, jumping over the bodies. Some people are so confused that they run sideways in their panic. Again we see the Richelieu statue and the Cossacks from the rear and then a travelling shot takes us down the steps from left to right as the crowd flees in parallel. Women, including the schoolmistress, crouch behind a low wall in fear. A long shot depicts a tree and rooftops as the crowd flees downwards, followed by closer shots of people crouching and collapsing. Another overhead shot of the Richelieu statue shows that the Cossacks are now well on their way down the steps. An officer treads on an elderly man lying dazed on the ground. An overhead shot depicts the chaos. A travelling shot, this time slightly ahead of the fleeing crowd, includes the young mother who had shown her son how to wave. The Cossacks fire and the boy falls on the steps. His mother is swept onward, again from left to right, by the fleeing crowd, unaware that he has fallen. A close-up shows the boy's bloodstained face as he shouts, 'Mama': the shot is so vivid that we almost hear him shout as well. The camera follows the mother down the steps to the next landing, when she realizes that her son is no longer with her, turns and looks back. We see the look of horror on her face as she realizes what has happened. The camera cuts to the boy, whose head drops to the ground. His mother presses her hands against her temples in shock and horror. The boy's limp and prostrate body is now being trampled by the crowd, still fleeing left to right. The frenzied mother advances towards the camera, her face filling the screen in extreme close-up. Further shots depict the crowd fleeing downwards left to right as the shocked mother slowly moves from right to left up the steps. These are intercut with images of hands, feet and even bodies, being trampled on in the panic flight. As the boy is trampled, his body rolls over like a rag doll. The mother approaches her son, her eyes filling the screen. She cradles her dead son in her arms and moves further up the steps towards the approaching Cossacks, while the crowd continues in downward flight around her. The mother stops, turns and shouts something to the crowd. This marks the point at which something like resistance to the Cossacks begins. It is a visually striking moment and a turning point.

The schoolmistress stands up and draws her shawl around her. The mother turns again and shouts. The schoolmistress calls to those around her and we see the title: 'Let us appeal to them!' Her companions cling to her skirts. The sequence that follows has its own symmetry: close-up of the schoolmistress; close-up of the group; long shot of the Cossacks descending left to right; long shot of the mother ascending right to left; close-up of the group; close-up of the schoolmistress. Her appeal has gone full circle: the group, including an elderly man on crutches, stand up and follow her. The Cossacks fire. A travelling shot once more shows the crowd fleeing from left to right, this time shot from behind, a device that increases the dynamism of the movement. Then we see the mother and son again moving in the opposite direction, cutting to the group around the schoolmistress and then back to the mother and son. The Cossacks advance, rifles at the ready, but this time their direction is different – still from left to right but this time from bottom left to top right. This device could well be another Eisensteinian *Vorschlag*, this time of the possibility of compromise. A rear-view shot shows the mother and son centre frame against a white strip of light up the middle of the steps. This strip of light is a device borrowed from religious paintings. In rear frame the Cossacks are visible descending towards the camera, with bodies strewn on either side. The moment of confrontation, the moment of truth, has arrived.

The mother ascends the centre strip of light shouting: 'Listen to me! Don't shoot!' A medium close-up shot shows the Cossacks still descending the steps from left to right but *upwards* across the frame: another *Vorschlag* of possible compromise serves to heighten the tension. A travelling front-angle shot shows the mother ascending right to left and then standing in the shadow of the Cossacks, an officer's sword raised above her. The next title explains: 'My boy is hurt!' The previous shot is repeated. The group round the schoolmistress advances, their arms outstretched in supplication. The officer gives the signal for the Cossacks to fire. For a moment the smoke from their rifles obscures the figure of the mother. As the smoke clears the mother falls slowly across screen to the ground. In the next shot fleeing civilians at the bottom of the steps are briefly blocked by two caval-rymen. Further up the steps the mother's body falls to the ground, her dead son spread-eagled across her chest. The next title finally informs

11. The Odessa Steps: 'My boy is hurt'

us that these merchants of death are 'Cossacks'. By this time the Russian audience would scarcely need to have been told, so the positioning of this intertitle shows Eisenstein once again 'holding back' to heighten the sense of tension and delay the unleashing of the full horror of the situation, because the Cossacks had an awesome reputation for their ruthless military skills and their horsemanship.[13]

The crowd rushes across the screen left to right at the bottom of the steps and we then see them descending the steps again. Cossack cavalrymen approach the bottom of the steps from the left, lashing out at the fleeing crowd, while the riflemen complete their descent, stepping over the corpses of the mother and son. We can see the corpses of innocent civilians strewn to the left and right of the action. In panic some people even throw themselves over the railings to avoid the advancing troops. The schoolmistress leads a small group of citizens to appeal to the troops. We see firing rifles cutting the screen diagonally from top left to bottom right, echoing the predominant direction of movement of both the fleeing crowd and the advancing troops. The group around the schoolmistress falls to the ground in fear, but she remains standing and imploring. The riflemen advance on the level from left to right.

At the top of one flight of steps a young mother in black moves from right to left, pushing a baby in a pram against the tide of humanity in flight. She hesitates at the hazardous descent before her and stops to fasten the baby securely. Civilians continue to flee past her down the steps: one of them, a young woman, accidentally knocks against the pram, the mother pushes her away and turns back to look at the advancing troops. Close-ups show her confused state of mind and the baby in its pram. The young mother places herself between the pram and the advancing riflemen to protect her baby, but this leaves nothing between the pram and the hazardous descent down the steps. She cries out as she realizes this. The next shot shows five empty steps: a line of black boots advances steadily downward left to right across both the steps and the screen. Against the sky we see the smoke of rifles fired. In extreme close-up the woman's head sways back as she writhes in agony: as she falls she nudges the pram gently backwards towards the top of the flight of steps, where it teeters on the edge. Further close-ups show her face in agony, and then her hands clutching the buckle on her belt. At the centre of this buckle is a representation of a white swan.

The swan has fulfilled a complex representative function in European mythology. In the classical period the swan was a symbol of

beauty associated with Venus/Aphrodite, the goddess of love and fertility, whose chariot was sometimes drawn by a pair of swans. It was
also a symbol of music and classical and later writers have maintained
that the swan emits a beautiful song at the moment of its death. In the
final scene of Shakespeare's *Othello*, for instance, Emilia's dying words
include the sentence, 'I will play the swan and die in music.'[14] This has
led the swan to be associated with Apollo, the sun-god and embodiment of the classical Greek spirit, who represented the rational and
civilized aspect of human nature (as opposed to Bacchus/Dionysus,
who represented the darker, more passionate aspect). Apollo dwelt on
Mount Olympus with the nine muses, the goddesses of the creative
arts. The swan was often particularly identified with Clio, the muse of
history, and Erato, the muse of lyric and love poetry. Furthermore,
classical mythology had it that Jupiter/Jove/Zeus, the supreme ruler of
the other gods and mortals, had impregnated Leda in the guise of a
swan, so the swan is also associated lastly with rape. Given Eisenstein's
belief at this time in the centrality of the montage of attractions, we
must assume that the swan on the buckle is intended to evoke all these
associations: beauty, fertility, love, music, reason and civilization,
creativity, history, but also rape.[15] The difficulty with this last association however is that in classical mythology it is the swan that commits
the rape, rather than being the defenceless victim of it. In *Potemkin*,
however, the young mother is clearly the victim of metaphorical collective rape by the advancing riflemen, acting as agents of the tsarist
system. Her fine clothing, the quality and wealth represented by both
the buckle and the pram, suggest that she is yet another middle-class
victim of the Cossack assault. That much would have been obvious to
contemporary mass audiences, although the mythological background
to the symbolism of the swan would certainly have passed them by.

The Cossack cavalry is seen flailing around at the base of the steps.
A close-up shows the young mother clutching her buckle, blood
dripping over her belt and gloved hands. In extreme close-up her head
sinks out of the frame. She falls out of view, leaving the baby in the
pram and the crowd fleeing past, this time right to left, in the
background. This momentary change of direction adds to the confusion and the tension. The pram edges towards the steps, the riflemen
advance down the steps, and the mother, clutching her stomach, finally
falls back, knocking the pram towards the top left of the frame into free
fall down the steps. At the bottom the cavalry continue their chaotic
battle with the fleeing civilians.

12. The Odessa Steps: the pram

The descent of the pram down the Odessa Steps is probably the most famous image in *The Battleship Potemkin*. The device of using the suffering of a child to move the audience has been much imitated, although Eisenstein, unlike so many of his imitators, leaves the sufferings of this particular baby to our imagination, rather than depicting it in graphic detail. The pram moves *upwards* to the left across the screen, although it is in fact moving *down* the steps. The schoolmistress sees what is happening to the helpless child and is appalled. Blood runs across her cheek and her hat and shawl have fallen away. The baby is now crying in the pram as it moves from left to right. A travelling shot accompanies the pram on its downward journey. The steps are littered with the dead and wounded. There are now more cavalrymen attacking the civilians at the bottom of the steps. The young mother in black now lies dead, sprawled across the steps, her head extending over the edge, just as the head of the young woman and her hair extend over the edge of the bridge being raised in Eisenstein's later film *October*. The pram moves on. In close-up we are shown the horrified expression on the schoolmistress's face: she is looking dishevelled and bloodied as she stares off-screen at the pram. A close-up shows the

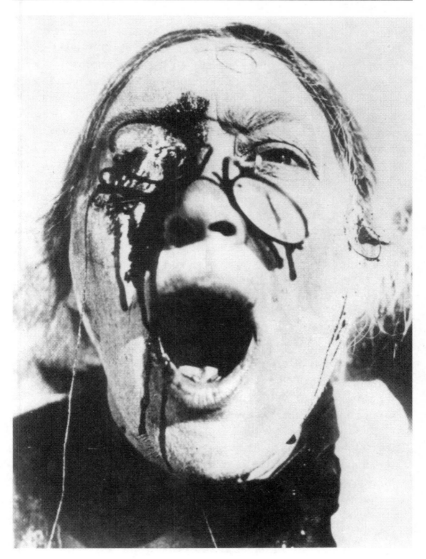

13. The Odessa Steps: the 'schoolmistress'

wheels of the pram as it descends from left to right. Another shows the face of a young man (typage suggests he is an archetypal student) as he notices in horror what is happening off-screen. At the side of the steps an elderly man stands up by the railings but is knocked down by the falling body of a woman. The pram now moves *upwards* across the frame. A close-up depicts the student with his face pressed close to a mirror as he watches. The pram rolls on, its progress watched by the real and reflected face of the student. In the pram the baby is being buffeted as it moves out of the frame from right to left. Confusion and helplessness are the order of the day. The boots of the riflemen, who are cut off by the upper frame, stand on the steps above the dead and dying. Two imploring hands stretch upwards from the bottom right of the screen. Rifles with fixed bayonets point downward at the bodies: the riflemen shoot. In extreme close-up the student screams and his face fills the screen. The pram continues downwards, rolling over an extended arm. From above we see the pram moving across a landing and then appearing to tip over. A Cossack slashes at the camera with his sabre and we see the vicious expression on his face in extreme close-up as he does this. The next shot is another extreme close-up, showing the face of the schoolmistress. Her pince-nez are now awry on her nose, the right lens shattered as her right eye bleeds. Her mouth gapes in horror. In his 1929 article 'The Dramaturgy of Film Form (The Dialectical Approach to Film Form)' Eisenstein cited this as an instance of 'logical montage':

> Representation of a spontaneous action, *Potemkin* (Fig. 1). Woman with pince-nez. Followed immediately – without a transition – by the same woman with shattered pince-nez and bleeding eye. Sensation of a shot hitting the eye.[16]

The schoolmistress too falls victim to the Cossacks and the image of her bloodied face (Eisensteinian *Nachschlag*) brings us back to, and contrasts with, the peaceful scenes before the massacre (Eisensteinian *Vorschlag*) when the townspeople of Odessa were standing on the quay side waving at the mutinous sailors to express their solidarity and support.

It is now the turn of the sailors to demonstrate their solidarity and support: from the bloodied face of the schoolmistress there is a dissolve to the gun-turret of the battleship. A giant cannon slowly rotates towards the camera from the right. A title tells us: 'The brutal military power answered by the guns of the battleship.' In another rather obvious studio shot the muzzles of two giant cannons point towards the camera, the bridge and superstructure visible in the background. The title explains: 'Target! The Odessa Theatre'. A close-up shows us a group of sculptures on the cupola of the theatre – a goddess and

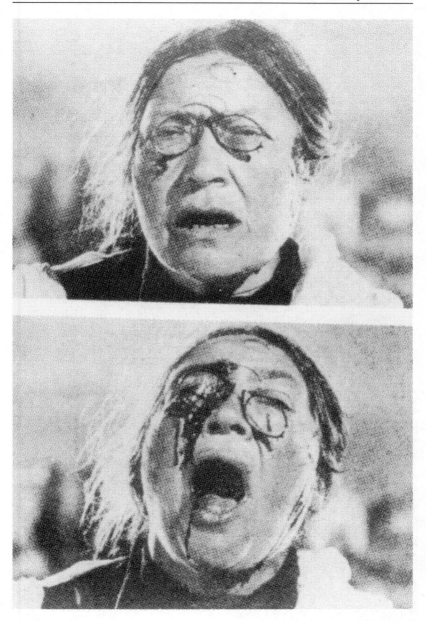

14. (a & b) Fig. 1: logical montage

chariot surrounded by leopards – silhouetted against the sky. The next title tells us that this is 'The headquarters of the generals!'. Once more the tsarist forces are abusing culture for their own ends by having commandeered the theatre (in actual fact, the opera house) as their *military* headquarters, taking us back to the *Vorschlag* of the officer trampling the piano towards the end of Part 1 of the film. The 'Potemkin' fires its guns. Three shots of the stone cherubs decorating the theatre suggest that they are startled and disturbed. An ornamental iron gate is hit by the 'Potemkin's' shell and begins to topple over. Smoke obscures the destruction. Three sculptured marble lions are shown in sequence. The first is asleep, the second has its head raised, and the third is fully alert and standing on its forelegs. In the same 1929 article Eisenstein cited this sequence as an example of 'alogical montage':

> This device used for symbolic pictorial expression. *Potemkin*. The marble lion leaps up, surrounded by the thunder of *Potemkin*'s guns firing in protest against the bloodbath on the Odessa Steps (Fig. 2).
> Cut together from three immobile marble lions at Alupka Castle (Crimea). One sleeping. One waking. One rising. The effect was

15. (a, b & c) Fig 2: alogical montage

achieved because the length of the middle piece was correctly calculated. Superimposition on the first piece produced the first jump. Time
for the second position to sink in. Superimposition of the third position on the second – the second jump. Finally the lion is standing.[17]

Symbolically, the spirit of revolution has awoken. Part 4 ends with
scenes of smoke and destruction.

Part 5: Meeting the Squadron

Following the massacre on the Odessa Steps, the audience might well
have expected the concluding section of *The Battleship Potemkin* to have
been characterized by an atmosphere of violent revenge and vicious
revolutionary bloodletting. Eisenstein, however, chose to end his film
differently. It may well be that he was to some extent bound by consid-
erations of historical accuracy although, given his re-creation of history
in both this film and elsewhere, this seems inherently improbable.
Nonetheless, Eisenstein, like other film-makers re-creating the events of
1905, was confronted by one major difficulty. In the short term the
'Revolution' of 1905 was not as 'revolutionary' as it was subsequently
portrayed to be: it ushered in a limited constitutional reform centred on
the creation of the State Duma, but there was no elemental change in
the political, economic or social systems and the *ancien régime* tottered
on for another dozen years. Eisenstein therefore had to portray what
was in the short term a defeat as a victory, as he had also had to do in
his previous film *The Strike* [Stachka, 1925], where the massacre was
followed by a call for vengeance. Faced with a somewhat similar
problem in *The Mother* [Mat', 1926], Vsevolod Pudovkin (who was
admittedly constrained by the ending to Maxim Gorky's original novel
on which the film was based) concluded with a reference to 1917, with
1905 as a staging post on the way to the ultimate victory of the Revolution. The historical 'Potemkin' sailed away to Constanța in Romania,
where many of the mutinous crew deserted, but the ship itself was
returned to tsarist Russia. This would have made far too ambiguous an
ending to the film version of events and Eisenstein cleverly set a revolutionary agenda that leads to a sense of liberation and hope, rather than
defeat and/or humiliation.

The final part of *Potemkin* opens with a suggestive title: 'Till evening
a stormy meeting went on.' We see a sailor, dressed in white uniform,
gesticulating against a background of the remaining crew framed by

two cannons pointing away from the camera. In previous shots the cannons have almost always been pointed at or near the camera, representing the threat of force of arms. Here, as they are pointing away from the camera, they serve to emphasize that the mutinous crew now has power over that force of arms. We deduce that the sailors are debating how best to use that power next. In medium close-up we see the gesticulating sailor again and a title tells us what he is saying: 'The people of Odessa await their deliverers. The citizens and soldiers will join you.' We return to the medium close-up, then to general shots of the sailors engaged in lively debate. Their options are now limited as the next title reminds us: 'Landing is impossible. The squadron is on its way.' The option of physically uniting with the citizens of Odessa is therefore no longer available. In long shot we see the battleship's quarterdeck. After further exchanges the men raise their caps and cheer. One doubting sailor succumbs to his comrades' persuasion. The title tells us: 'With one vote they decided to meet the squadron.' In the crow's nest and on the quarterdeck the cheer goes up. The latter shot dissolves to an empty deck and then fades out completely to darkness and the title: 'The night came, full of anxieties.'

The St Andrew's cross, the ensign of the Russian navy seen early in Part 2, is lowered between the cannons at the stern against the evening sky. The sun sets over the sea in a series of shots that evoke the calm and peaceful, yet tense and ominous, atmosphere associated with the earlier mourning for Vakulinchuk, the first martyr of the 'Potemkin' mutiny. A sequence of shots cuts first to a sailing boat, like those in the harbour during the earlier nocturnal mourning for the fallen hero, then to the sun, and later presumably also the moon, reflected on the calm surface of the sea. If the massacre on the Odessa Steps is the new thesis, and this surface calm the new antithesis, the new synthesis of the anticipated confrontation is soon to emerge, for, underneath the surface calm, there is both turbulence and fear. We cut to the night watch, and then back to the waves crashing against the shore, as at the beginning of the film, suggesting once more the threat of an impending storm and thus raising tension among the audience. The rather unconvincing model of the 'Potemkin' from the Sandunov Baths is seen briefly in a tank representing a calm sea: 'Potemkin' rides at anchor, silhouetted against the evening sky. In the engine room two large dials stand at zero: this is the relative calm before the storm. The camera cuts from a sailor asleep in his bunk to another on watch and then to a searchlight seeking out the rest of the tsarist fleet. A close-up of darting spots of light reflected on the surface of the sea suggests fragmentation, disarray and chaos. But a long shot places these darting spots in context, 'explaining' them and immediately restoring a sense of order and calm. There is a series of routine intercut shots of a battleship at sea: Matiushenko (another link back to Vakulinchuk) wakes and stubs out a cigarette; the ship sails on through the waves, a plume of smoke stretching into the distance; the bunks; the searchlight ceaselessly revolving; the engine room; the bridge, with Matiushenko giving orders; men sleeping; men on watch; the dials in the engine room; the watch again; a rotating rangefinder; the gun; the rangefinder again; and finally the growing tension is broken by the sighting of a ship on the horizon. The title proclaims: 'Enemy sighted!' The assumption that the tsarist fleet is the 'enemy', rather than that the men on board the other ships are 'brothers', immediately sets the scene for confrontation and heightens the tension.

Once more we are shown a sailor cleaning a cannon: this time he appears to be polishing the outside instead of the inside of the barrel in what could be interpreted as a masturbatory gesture, albeit a fleeting one. The sailor leaves his cannon and from below we see sailors running across the grille as in the sequence in Part 1 leading up to the mutiny. This time there are no officers to order them about and below deck it is the sailors who wake their comrades while, up on deck, other sailors move to their stations. The lookout peers through his rangefinder. The next title conveys the gist of this activity: 'All hands on deck!' At the sound of a bugle the sailors scramble on deck 'To battle stations!' Another sequence of intercut shots includes the bugler; the scrambling to stations; the engine room; ammunition being rolled out; the decks in preparation; the embarkation ladder is hauled up to prevent boarding; the dials – all these preparations are to prepare the ship for battle. Shells are laid out on the very tarpaulin used by the officers to cover the mutineers prior to the unsuccessful order to shoot, emphasizing once more that it is those same sailors who are now in control of the ship, if not necessarily of events. All the time the tension is palpably rising.

The next title confirms what we have already suspected: 'Full speed ahead!' The final decision has been taken to confront the fleet. Another sequence of rapid cutting shows us Matiushenko on the bridge giving orders; pistons in the engine room moving at an accelerating pace; smoke billowing from the battleship's funnels; the ship's wake trailing away in the sea. The battleship moves forward through the water at increasing speed, the cannons are prepared for use and the tension mounts rhythmically towards the climax. The title tells us that the ship is now at 'Top speed' and a downward shot shows us the ship's prow cutting forward through the sea.

In long shot we see the squadron sailing towards 'Potemkin'. In accelerating cuts we see the same images as before of cannons, pistons, sea and smoke. A long shot depicts 'The Potemkin and Torpedo-Boat 267' (which historically did escort the mutinous battleship) sailing in parallel to confront the 'enemy'. On the bridge the message is clear: 'The flagship is advancing!' Eisenstein used old newsreel footage for some of the following shots, rather than filming them afresh: constraints of time and money left him with little alternative, but the use of this footage does serve to blur the distinction made by purists then and since between 'fiction' and 'documentary' footage. We see the fleet front-end on and approaching: more shots follow of smoke, sea and guns. The title proclaims: 'The squadron is nearing us!' and this is immediately confirmed by the images that follow. One shot looks back to the smoke trail that 'Potemkin' is leaving in its wake, as if to suggest that it is leaving the safety of Odessa and sailing into the unknown in its confrontation with the squadron.

Matiushenko issues a challenge: 'Run up the signal. Don't fight – join us!' Silhouetted against the sky the flagman signals the approaching ships: 'Join ... us!' Between the titles showing these two words we see the battleship's signal flags spelling out the same message, the halyards stretching from the deck to the top of the mast. There is more rapid intercutting between shots of the sea, the smoke, the gun silhouetted against the sky, the sailors. Now 'The enemy is within range.' A sailor cradles a shell. The next title comments: 'All for one'. The gun-turret rotates to face the camera in a threatening gesture that further increases the tension. Coiled ropes lie in readiness on the deck. The gun-turret rises to herald the climax of the action. A close-up shows the raised gun with the ship's mast in the background. The previous title is inverted: 'One for all.'

Above the mutinous battleship the red flag flies. We know that, when *The Battleship Potemkin* was first shown, the earlier shots of the red flag were actually hand-coloured in red. Some subsequent prints have also coloured the flag red at this point but there is no direct historical evidence for this, although the general sense of reference back to earlier key elements in the film would seem to support the case for colouring here too. Indeed, this is one of the many devices by which Eisenstein was able to turn *real* defeat into *reel* victory.

As the confrontation nears, there are further shots of the cannons, the engine room and the fleet, all the key elements in this final act of the drama. Sailors give valedictory hugs to one another, anticipating battle, defeat and possible death. A rising cannon fills the screen and this is followed by further shots of the engine room, the gun-turret, the ropes on the deck, and the cannon, leading to the title: 'Will they fire?' The sailors' faces are shown in extreme close-up, and then a cannon, followed by the first doubts: '... or...'. Another montage shows faces, cannons, the ship in long shot, shells, faces again. As the pace slows, the tension begins to subside and one of the sailors smiles as he realizes that Matiushenko's gamble has worked and that there is not going to be a confrontation with the 'enemy' after all. The title proclaims: 'BROTHERS!' and a close-up of the sailors cheering follows. They swarm on to the quarterdeck and across the grating that we have seen several times before. They cheer as the red flag appears again and the guns are lowered as they wave at the passing squadron. A travelling shot takes us round the bow of 'Potemkin'. The deck is crammed with cheering sailors: 'Over the heads of the tsarist admirals roared a brotherly cheer.' The final montage sequence of the film shows the bows of the ship, the cheering sailors, the deck, the crow's nest, the smoke from the stacks, the flag on the mast, all intercut with one another.

In the final shot of *The Battleship Potemkin* we see a view from below of the ship's prow driving straight upwards across the screen towards the camera. It first cuts the screen in two and then continues to burst beyond the screen space – implicitly at least – into the auditorium, overrunning the audience and carrying the mutinous sailors to freedom. Eisenstein has here played with the effects achieved by the Lumière brothers in 1895 with their famous depiction of a train at La Ciotat station in the south of France. The film is known as *The Arrival of the Train in the Station* but the cameraman was positioned half-way along the platform so that, as the train came to a halt, it passed beyond the left-hand outer edge of the screen causing a sensation, as the Russian writer Maxim Gorky recalled in his syndicated newspaper column:

A railway train appears on the screen. It darts like an arrow straight towards you – look out! It seems as if it is about to rush into the darkness in which you are sitting and reduce you to a mangled sack of skin, full of crumpled flesh and shattered bones, and destroy this hall and this building, so full of wine, women, music and vice, and transform it into fragments and to dust.[18]

16. The final scene: the battleship 'escapes' into the audience, instead of to Romania

The effect of the Lumière film was accidental: the effect of Eisenstein's device was of course intentional, and it is on this dramatic escape from the confines of the film frame that *The Battleship Potemkin* comes triumphantly to 'THE END'.

Themes and Variations

In this short section I want merely to point to a small number of the very many points that *The Battleship Potemkin* raises for further discussion and analysis. The first of these is the matter of the film's historical authenticity, which, as we shall see in the section on *Reception*, provided the focus for many of the criticisms made both within the USSR and abroad. The differences between the real events of the actual mutiny in 1905 and the reel re-creation of those events in the film have been the subject of both a book by Richard Hough and an article by Charles Wenden.[19] Unfortunately neither source is annotated to today's scholarly standards but perhaps that does not really matter because, as Hough quite rightly argues, the question of authenticity is something of a (very, in this case) red herring:

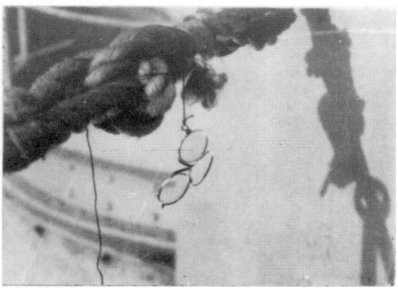

Time, and propaganda, have so clouded the truth of the 'Potemkin'
mutiny that it must surely be among the most inaccurately recorded
events in naval history. Present Russian accounts, and even descrip-
tions of the event written by the same eye-witness on different occa-

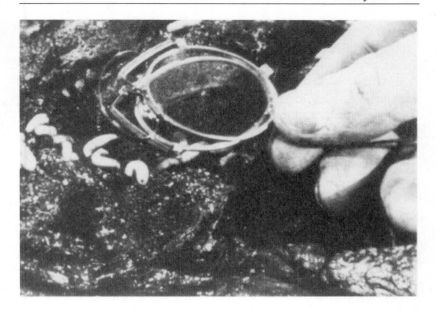

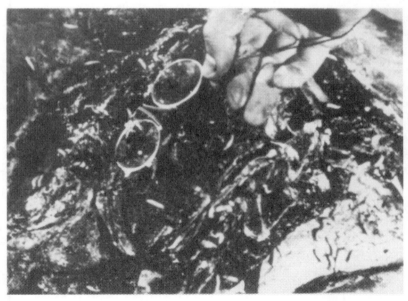

17. (a, b, c & d) The pince-nez as signifier: seeing and not seeing, being and not being

sions, are at variance in detail; and none of these tally precisely with those of officers of the Black Sea Fleet who are alive today. The chief difficulty is that ... it has already attained legendary status in the USSR, with the battleship as a sacred memorial and Afanasy Matushenko as a revered martyr of the 1905 revolution. To émigré Russian officers memories of the incident are naturally coloured in some degree by shame and indignation; and it is as foolish to expect the Soviet version to be any more accurate than a Tudor rendering of the Battle of Bosworth.[20]

In other words, there is nothing new under the sun: this device we call poetic licence. If Shakespeare was doing it, why should not Eisenstein?

One of the characteristic features of *Potemkin* is the application of Eisenstein's principle of the montage of attractions. Objects are chosen for associations that will resonate with the audience. There are many examples, but I want to highlight the idea of 'seeing' because it provides an instance of the ways in which Eisenstein plays with the different associations that a single object has for the spectator. Let us take the pince-nez. These are first seen on the nose of the doctor examining the rotten meat in the first part of the film. Throughout the film pince-nez denote a middle-class character, hence the ambiguity of the signifier. What should be an aid to seeing becomes, in the case of the doctor, an aid to blindness, particularly when he doubles the pince-nez back on themselves in order to magnify the rotten meat. When he is thrown overboard, his pince-nez are left hanging on the ship-side ropes as a symbol (much imitated later – in Hitchcock's *Strangers on a Train* [USA, 1951], for example) of his demise. Yet, when the 'schoolmistress' on the Odessa Steps wears pince-nez, these represent her clarity of vision: hence, to restore the 'proper order of society' the Cossack has to slash, not just her face, but also her pince-nez, in order to destroy both her vision and her life. Elsewhere, one of the women with a parasol peers through a lorgnette, another symbol of the bourgeoisie, but here this is also a visual aid helping her to see reel reality. Although for Eisenstein seeing was not always believing, seeing does at least provide the opportunity of determining the truth. Hence, *in the film*, Captain Golikov's need to cover the mutineers with a tarpaulin before they are to be shot. According to memoir materials *in historical reality* the tarpaulin was spread on the deck to prevent it being stained with blood. On the other hand we see Giliarovsky's eye in close-up before he fires the fatal shot at Vakulinchuk: here we are seeing *inside* the officer's mind, perhaps, rather than considering his view *outwards*.

Other signifiers and factors worth further examination include:

- the unambiguously class-defining parasols and clothing,
- the relationship between the individual and the crowd,
- the role and identity of the 'hero' of the film: is it the mutinous crew, the townspeople of Odessa, or the battleship itself?
- the relationship between land and water, as exemplified by the crew and the townspeople,
- the gender relationship between men and women in the film,
- the sexual connotations of some of the imagery, especially the role of the battleship's cannons,
- the antithesis between light and dark, black and white as overall signifiers of good and evil,
- the direction of movement in the various episodes in the film: up-down, right-left, vertical-horizontal-diagonal.

It is only through a more exhaustive examination of these and other aspects of *The Battleship Potemkin* that we shall eventually come to a greater understanding of the power and significance of Eisenstein's film. But, as that 1926 *Izvestiia* review predicted, 'This film will be studied for a long time.'

Notes

1 Cited by Leonid Kozlov in: K & L, p. 345.
2 D. Bordwell, *The Cinema of Eisenstein*, Cambridge MA, 1993, p. 64.
3 A. Gvozdev, 'Novaia pobeda sovetskogo kino. (*Bronenosets Potemkin* i "Teatral'nyi Oktiabr')', *Zhizn iskusstva* (Leningrad), 26 January 1926, pp. 7–8; translated as 'A New Triumph for Soviet Cinema (*The Battleship Potemkin* and the "Theatrical October"'' in: *FF*, pp. 140–3; cf. Marshall, pp. 239–44
4 This is a paraphrase of Lenin's observation:

Revolution is war. Of all the wars known in history it is the only lawful, rightful, just and truly great war ... All detached observers now are of one accord in admitting that in Russia this war has been declared and begun.

This comes from 'The Plan of the St Petersburg Battle', the third part of 'Revolutionary Days', first published in *Vpered*, 18 January 1905, and translated in: V.I. Lenin, *Collected Works. Vol. 8: January–July 1905*, Moscow, 1962, p. 107.

5   The original Count Grigori Potemkin was one of Catherine the Great's favourites. He had allegedly tried to impress her by ordering the construction of sham villages in order to give a false impression of rural prosperity when she toured the Crimea in 1787, hence the term 'Potemkin villages'.
6   Matthew, 6:11.
7   J. Goodwin, *Eisenstein, Cinema and History*, Urbana IL, 1993, p. 62; *ESW4*, p. 155; and Bordwell, pp. 63–4, respectively.
8   D. Mayer, *Sergei M. Eisenstein s 'Potemkin. A Shot-by-Shot Presentation*, New York, 1989, p. 91. This is shot 381 in Mayer's account.
9   *ESW4*, p. 158.
10 A Chaldean was originally an inhabitant of Chaldea or a member of the governing elite of ancient Babylon, but the term has come to be synonymous with an astrologer or practitioner of the occult or, as here, a general term of abuse for someone who is not a 'true believer'.
11 The German *Vorschlag* denotes a musical 'forestroke', an auxiliary note that anticipates and merges in performance with the principal note.
12 S. M. Eisenstein [Eizenshtein], '"E!" O chistote kinoiazyka', *Sovetskoe kino*, May 1934, pp. 25–31, translated as ' "Eh!" On the Purity of Film Language' in: S. M. Eisenstein, *Selected Works. Vol. 1: Writings, 1922–34*, London and Bloomington IN, 1988 [hereafter *ESW1*], pp. 285–95; R. Taylor (ed.), *The Eisenstein Reader,* [hereafter *ER*], London, 1998, pp. 124–33.
13 The Cossacks also appear as the 'Wild Division' in Eisenstein's film made to mark the tenth anniversary of the 1917 Revolution, *October* [Oktiabr', 1927].
14 W. Shakespeare, *Othello*, act 5, scene 2, ll. 247–8.
15 See the relevant entries in: J. Hall, *Dictionary of Subjects and Symbols in Art*, London, 1979.
16 *ESW1*, pp. 171–2; *ER*, pp. 102–3.
17 *ESW1*, pp. 172–4; *ER*, pp. 103–4.
18 'I. M. Pacatus' [Maxim Gorky], 'Beglye zametki. Sinematograf Lium'era', *Nizhegorodskii listok*, 4 July 1896, translated as 'The Lumière Cinematograph' in: *FF*, pp. 25–6.
19 R. Hough, *The Potemkin Mutiny*, London, 1960; D. J. Wenden, '*Battleship Potemkin* Film and Reality', in: K. R. M. Short (ed.), *Feature Films as History*, London, 1981, pp. 37–61.
20 Hough, p. 9.

3. Reception

The final version of *The Battleship Potemkin* was released on 18 January 1926 and premiered at two cinemas in central Moscow, the Metropole and the Art (Khudozhestvennyi), also known as the First Goskino Theatre.[1] Both cinemas were decked out like battleships and all the theatre staff wore naval uniform.[2] The film was also shown from 19 January at a dozen or so other cinemas in the capital and billed as 'the pride of Soviet cinema'.[3] The audience figures for *Potemkin* were compared in the press with those for the American film *Robin Hood*, starring Douglas Fairbanks, which had recently been released in the Soviet Union. The comparison was billed as a battle between the USA and the USSR, between capitalist and socialist culture. One trade paper produced figures to show that in the First Goskino Theatre 29,458 people had seen *Potemkin* in a twelve-day period while 'only' 21,281 had seen *Robin Hood*, while in the Second Goskino Theatre the figures were 39,405 and 33,960 respectively.[4] In its advertisements in February 1926 the First Goskino Theatre claimed that in its first four weeks '300,000 people had seen the pride of Soviet cinema'.[5]

There are, of course, lies, damned lies and statistics. Despite these statistics *Potemkin* was taken off on 16 February, while the earlier claim that 'All Moscow is watching *Robin Hood*' seemed to be justified after all as the American film continued to play until the summer 'by popular demand'.[6] Indeed, when *Potemkin* returned to Moscow screens after its triumph in Berlin it both displaced, and was replaced by, *Robin Hood*. Eisenstein's film does seem to have had some popular success on the workers' film circuit, where facilities were basic and seat prices low. But, in commercial cinemas (many of which were, ironically, owned by public organizations such as trade unions or local authorities), where people had to pay more for their seats, it had to be sold hard. As we shall see, *Potemkin* was a phenomenal success in Berlin and it

18. The *Potemkin* premiere in Moscow, January 1926

was there that it was shown, in the midst of their European tour, to Douglas Fairbanks and Mary Pickford,[7] the latter at that time was not merely 'America's sweetheart' but also Soviet Russia's. The German Communist Party newspaper *Die rote Fahne* reported:

> After the performance they were surrounded by German and foreign journalists and correspondents. They were all asking the famous Hollywood actor for his opinion of Eisenstein's film. Douglas Fairbanks said: '*The Battleship Potemkin* is the most powerful and profound experience of my life.' Mary Pickford made her excuses because she was in no state to say anything. The film had made such a strong impression on her that she was crying.[8]

Their positive reaction was used to sell the film to Soviet audiences and wean them off their addiction to Hollywood.[9] Indeed Eisenstein acted as their guide when Doug and Mary visited Moscow in July 1926, showing them round the Kremlin and taking them to see Pudovkin's *The Mother*. During this visit Doug is reputed to have said to Eisenstein:

'I am surprised at the success of my weakest films, *The Thief of*

19. Tisse, Douglas Fairbanks and Eisenstein, Moscow, July 1926

Bagdad and *The Mark of Zorro* in Russia. Compared with your magnificent *The Battleship Potemkin*, these films do not deserve attention.'[10]

Eisenstein responded simply, 'But we love you' and, when *Potemkin* returned to Soviet screens in the summer of 1926, it was sold to Soviet audiences as a foreign hit.

The question of *Potemkin*'s relative success or failure with contemporary Soviet audiences is however complicated by several factors. The First Goskino Theatre had negotiated an exclusive exhibition licence that made it relatively expensive for other commercial cinemas to show the film. The country had limited reserves of foreign currency and had still to import all the raw materials necessary to make films and duplicate them: hence, presumably, the sale of the negative. In the mid-1920s Soviet cinema was still run along commercial lines and, despite official approval for *Potemkin*, not enough copies of the film were made for its general release throughout the country. Its distribution was therefore limited in the first instance to the larger cities. Furthermore there had been a trade war between the Russian and Ukrainian cinema organizations which had largely refused to distribute one another's films. One paper claimed that in 1926 the film was showing at more cinemas in Berlin than in the whole of the USSR put together.[11] Some sources claim that *The Battleship Potemkin* was not shown in Odessa, for example, until 1927,[12] but Eisenstein received a telegram from the city on 7 September 1926 telling him that the film was showing in three cinemas and was an 'unparalleled triumph'.[13] Two days later the Odessa evening paper reported that a gang of thieves had gained entry to one of these cinemas through the roof at three o'clock in the morning in a vain attempt to steal a copy of this film, which it described as 'sensational'.[14]

Under the title 'Goskino's Mistake' the Leningrad newspaper *Krasnaia gazeta* lamented in October 1926:

Who would have thought that the only film genuinely worthy of our Soviet country, *The Battleship Potemkin*, would have met a fate like this?

Potemkin, after triumphantly surpassing all its enemies – the talentless films ... denounced by our press right and left – has been unable to reach the Soviet spectator ... but has escaped, just like its great predecessor, not to the shores of Romania, but to be 'stranded' in the clutches of German cinema entrepreneurs. In short, success abroad so turned the heads of our film dealers that, without thinking, they sold the negative abroad, to Germany, retaining only the right to receive copies.

Meanwhile the limited number of copies we have in the USSR is wearing out and the best of them are only 40 per cent serviceable.

We cannot resume showing the film in workers' clubs, as they persistently demand. By showing these copies to visiting workers' delegations we consistently demonstrate what we are capable of, and how capable we are of spoiling the good that we have achieved.

Our foreign comrades, having watched our 40 per cent serviceable *Potemkin*, will admire our directors, cameramen and actors, but they will doubtless find a sufficient number of appropriate expressions for our bunglers. The promised copies from abroad have not arrived. To think that we have to wait for copies of the best Soviet film from abroad.[15]

If the popular reception of *Potemkin* at that time was ambiguous, so too was the reaction of contemporary critics and film-makers, especially inside the Soviet Union, where the sound of axes grinding was all too clearly audible.

It is worth noting that even the earliest reactions to Eisenstein's film raised most of the principal issues that were to be debated in subsequent decades: the question of historical authenticity; the relative roles of montage (and especially the montage of attractions) and acting; of the mass and the individual; the film's contribution to the determination of cinema's specificity; the nature, method and purpose of revolutionary art; the identity of the film's hero (was it the battleship itself, the mutinous crew, the citizens of Odessa or a combination of all three?); and the manner in which that heroism was conveyed to the audience. At one end of the spectrum were the enthusiasts, those who felt that Eisenstein and his team really had found a new mode of expression suited to the new revolutionary circumstances. Typical of these was Nikolai Volkov, who reviewed *Potemkin* for the newspaper *Trud* [Labour], the organ of the trades union movement, on New Year's Day 1926, in ecstatic terms. He began with the announcement that 'Here at last is a real victory for Soviet cinema; here at last is a genuine work of contemporary cinema art whose perfection is profoundly moving.' His review continued:

We must not make petty historical demands on *Potemkin*. It may

well be that the mutiny on the 'Potemkin' did not take place exactly as portrayed on screen.

But what does this matter when the director *Eisenstein*, in collaboration with his cameraman *Tisse*, has managed to express the very *spirit* of the revolution, its profound *dynamics*, its gigantic *rhythm*?

Everything comes alive in the hands of these superlative masters of the

20. (a, b, c & d) Contemporary Russian advertisements for *Potemkin*

screen – the sea, the battleship itself, the Odessa Steps, the white-winged skiffs, the human masses, the worms on the meat.

With amazing keenness Eisenstein observes nature, the human face, the machine. He listens with sensitivity to the very breathing of the ocean's depths. He loves material objects. He knows that revolution *is not an individual but the mass* and he is searching for the language to express mass emotions.

In this process everything is taken into account and weighed in the balance. The montage is just like a steel hoop, so masterfully and closely does it encompass each detail. The spectator can offer no resistance to the triumphant flow of impressions because Eisenstein knows when and how to employ each particular means of influence.

What photographic effects Tisse has extracted from the filming, what tenderness in the night shots, what fantasy in those ships sleeping on the nocturnal water.

Here is something to show to both the near and the far West. Of course *The Battleship Potemkin* demands the most intensive study. But what joy to witness the fact that the hopes raised by *The Strike* have not been in vain, that *The Strike* was the *first victory* and that it has been followed by such a *brilliant second.*

Before our very eyes Eisenstein is confidently entering the ranks of *world* film directors.[16]

In the film journal *Sovetskii ekran* [Soviet Screen] the critic Nikolai Aseyev was equally enthusiastic. He praised *Potemkin* as 'an enormous and genuine victory'. Eisenstein's film had ensured that:

A new hero has been introduced into the consciousness of the spectator. This hero is neither allegorical nor conventional, nor fetishistically sickly sweet. This hero is real and overwhelming in its authenticity, in the power of its renewed forms, and convincing in its life-like realism.

This hero is the revolutionary battleship, submitting to the sailors' will, cleansing itself of the scum of traditional privileges, the deadly conventionalism of enforced discipline, and with a free heart making the fresh sea froth up.[17]

Aseyev went on to praise Eisenstein for his attention to detail.

Lastly, everyday life on the battleship – the hold, the mess, the gun turret, the machines working, the deck – is all shown clearly and precisely, not just as background, 'as decoration'. No, everything lives and breathes because of the part it plays in the development of the action. The spectator sees the battleship both inside and out.

And, once he has familiarized himself with the minutest details of the scene of the action, the action itself begins to unfold. But what does it consist of?...

On the whole, of course, it consists of the details that are not immediately discernible to the spectator, the details that provoke a particular emotion, operating not only with the eye, but also through it.

It is from these details that the texture (*faktura*) of the film derives.

The details that Aseyev listed included: the way in which the sea and the sea mist are photographed, the grieving faces around the tent where Vakulinchuk lies in state, the candle in his hands, the boats taking provisions to the battleship, and the baby in the pram rolling down the Odessa Steps. 'All these,' he claimed, 'represent an accumulation of details that alone give the action plausibility.'

In the same month, January 1926, the anonymous 'Correspondent' (*Primechatel*) of the Moscow evening newspaper *Vecherniaia Moskva* compared *Potemkin* to *The Birth of A Nation*:

This film is an event. Just as Griffith's *Birth of A Nation* initiated the great American cinema, so this second work by Eisenstein initiates *the great Soviet cinema*.

Soviet cinema has already achieved a great deal. It has many undoubted successes to its name. But has it really yet acquired its own identity?

We have done a great deal to assimilate the culture of bourgeois cinema. We have assiduously adapted the forms found in American and European nurseries to our own conditions.

In a word, we have *learnt*. We shall go on learning for a long time: that is unavoidable.

But now, after *Potemkin*, we shall remember *our own perspective*. Our own eventual goal. Our Soviet cinema, which will have its own identity, which does not repeat stereotyped petty-bourgeois patterns.

Cinema, like every art form, consists of more than its subject matter. It does not take much to introduce *Soviet subject matter* into our cinema. But we also have to produce our own ideas on how raw material should be treated – our own style.

Eisenstein's latest work decisively poses the question of our own style in cinema. This film was kneaded from the dough of great culture. But this is not a matter of assimilating culture passively, but of profoundly mastering it. *In this instance culture has been forced to serve new aims.*[18]

The anonymous 'Correspondent' concluded by remarking, 'How magnificent the whole film is and how clearly it defines the identity of Soviet cinema.'

On the same day another anonymous critic, writing in *Kinogazeta*, compared Eisenstein's *Potemkin* with another anniversary film, Viacheslav Viskovsky's *The Ninth of January* [Deviatoe ianvaria], devoted to the events of January 1905 that had become known as 'Bloody Sunday'. The comparison between these two films was an obvious one, and one that others were to make to Eisenstein's advantage.[19] Taking as his starting point the slogan of 'social command' (*sotsial nyi zakaz*), which was to assume greater importance as the decade wore on, the *Kinogazeta* critic argued that fulfilment of this command was not just a matter of who had commissioned the film:

These days 'social command' is a modish expression. So modish that it is already beginning to lose its true meaning and serve as a justification for that social evil, hackwork (*khaltura*).

Two pictures have been made from the cycle *The Year 1905*: Eisenstein's *The Battleship Potemkin* and Viskovsky's *The Ninth of January*. Do we really mean by 'social command' merely an order from a state institution? That would be a great mistake.

Yes, in his film Eisenstein does fulfil the social command, but not because he was working to government order. The social command does not derive from a studio director's office or a government commission. Eisenstein derived his social command from the proletarian revolution in which he emerged as an artist. The social command was not presented to him in the shape of a proposal to make a film. It grew within him as part of the organic process of development of both the revolution and of Eisenstein.

We believe that, even if Eisenstein's next film were not made to government order and not based on a script devoted to a revolutionary theme, Eisenstein would nevertheless fulfil the social command of the proletariat.[20]

One of the most significant of the early reviews of *Potemkin* appeared on 20 January 1926 – in other words two days after its Moscow release – in the Leningrad paper *Krasnaia gazeta*, which was later that year to highlight the distribution problems with the film. It was written by Adrian Piotrovsky, who was at that time a classicist, translator, critic, theorist and scriptwriter, but later an influential teacher and from 1928 to 1937 firstly Head of the Script Department, then Artistic Director, and finally Deputy Director of the Leningrad studios.[21] Piotrovsky was the first critic to appreciate the centrality of the Odessa Steps sequence, describing it as 'a genuine staircase into Hell, real steps of horror', and his article is cited here in full:

A worker, a student, a woman in a shawl, a clerk, a schoolboy – the hearts of the whole motley Soviet public move with a single emotion, a single indignation, anger, hope or pride. A work of art has rarely been so omnipotent, but it was just like that at the showing of *The Battleship Potemkin*, the first part of Eisenstein's epic on 1905. The impressive force of this film, which is not at all agitational but simply made by a brilliant artist and revolutionary, is so staggering that it seems at first as if this strict alternation of simple pictures has not been devised by anyone, as if a broad heroic life is rolling over us and can roll in no other way.

In fact this is a work of the most refined mastery and, more than that, it is a new kind of cinema art, a masterpiece of Soviet film style. As in his first picture, *The Strike*, Eisenstein seems to give new life to objects and people, showing them from quite unexpected and cleverly selected points of view. *Potemkin* is an amazing review of the men and the objects of the sea. The *contre-jour* photographs of the port of Odessa are the height of marine lyricism but this is far from being the most important thing. The shots in this film are locked into sequences, into 'parts' elevated by a pathos that is both great and pure. The indignation, the mutiny, the heroic grief for the dead man, the monstrous tsarist revenge, the extreme tension of waiting (the approach of the government squadron), the boundless rejoicing: these are the six emotional blocks that make up this poem and each block divides into hundreds of crystal-like shots, criss-crossing details, human faces, machine fragments, that are pierced through and through with a single burst of will characteristic of a particular part as a whole, and driven by an ever increasing tempo. The montage of pure pathos is Eisenstein's basic method.

That is why his *Potemkin* is monumental. The everyday precision, the authenticity of the stripes and badges that is favoured by others, left him virtually unmoved. *Potemkin*, Odessa: these are, in generalized terms, a mutinous battleship stirring a city. That is why the effect of his 'Odessa Steps' sequence is so irresistible: the wide white steps down which the crowd, pursued by gendarmes, runs, slides and cowers – a genuine staircase into Hell, real steps of horror. That is why your heart sinks when you see the solitary guns of the mutinous ship. For all its terrible concreteness and its absolute vitality, Eisenstein's art is symbolic and it is great enough to act like gigantic generalizations.

Does *Potemkin* have a plot? Yes, more so than *The Strike* – or, rather, the development of the pathos is here more firmly grounded and linked. But this crystal-clear and tremendously gripping plot unfolds without any intervention from the individual intrigue and personal romance that others consider necessary to a film. The hero is the sailors' battleship, the Odessa crowd, but characteristic figures are snatched here and there from the crowd. For a moment, like a conjuring trick, they attract all the sympathies of the audience: like the sailor Vakulinchuk, like the young woman and child on the Odessa Steps, but they emerge only to dissolve once more into the mass. This signifies: no film stars but a film of real-life types. It is as if the director is letting our eyes roam through the crowd: 'Look how rich simple life is!'

But the more public value of *Potemkin* cannot yet be measured. With it the first stone of a heroic epic of the revolution is laid, an epic that is like the daily bread of popular education in our country. It would be rash to leave this monumental fragment on its own. Stone by stone, by precisely these simple and sublime methods, we must make a film epic, a glorious monument to Soviet film style. Glory to Soviet cinema![22]

It was by no means unusual for Soviet critics in the 1920s to praise the work of one director at the expense of others, but Piotrovsky avoided such partisanship. Answering his own calls for a Soviet film style that did not 'leave this monumental fragment on its own' he claimed in a review of Vsevolod Pudovkin's *The Mother* in the same Leningrad newspaper in October 1926 that '*Potemkin* and *The Mother* – this is already a film style!'[23]

The other most significant review of January 1926 was also published in Leningrad, this time in the journal *Zhizn iskusstva* [Artistic Life]. In it Alexei Gvozdev, scholar and doyen of Leningrad theatre critics,[24] argued that those who saw in *Potemkin* an assertion of cinema specificity at the expense of theatre were misguided: the film constituted a rejection of the conventions of traditional 'academic' theatre, but a triumphant confirmation of the methods of the new revolutionary theatre characterized by the work of Vsevolod Meyerhold under the banner of 'Theatrical October'.[25] Under the heading 'A New Triumph for Soviet Cinema' Gvozdev began by recognizing that '*Potemkin* is an event of enormous public significance because in it form and content have been fused into a powerful unity and a film with a revolutionary theme has found its proper revolutionary artistic form.'[26]

Gvozdev went on to put the case for *Potemkin* as an example of the specificity of cinema before demolishing it:

People have said of *Potemkin* that its uniqueness lies in the fact that it represents a rejection of the methods of theatre and an affirmation of the specific methods of cinema. It is true, in fact, that there are no actors in the usual sense of the word. There is no theatrical 'hero' with his experiences in high society, no love melodrama, none of the sentimentalism or psychologism that permeate theatre and its off-spring – cinema of the usual kind. At the beginning of the film we see the beating of the waves, and the rhythm of the sea then develops in the following frames, concealing with growing strength the energy that is contained in the beating and movement of the waves. In theatre this would be impossible ... In Eisenstein's film it is objects and not actor 'heroes' that act: the battleship with its machinery, its staircases, the muzzles of its guns, or the city with its jetty, its bridges, streets and terraces. This would also be impossible in theatre.

Gvozdev then characterized what he termed the '*old* theatre' and agreed with those who argued that 'Eisenstein is far removed from all this.' But he then went on to argue for a continuity between the new theatre associated with Meyerhold and *Potemkin*:

But Eisenstein and his *Potemkin* are close blood relatives of the young art of the revolutionary years and, in particular, of the revolutionary years of the 'Theatrical October'. *Potemkin* represents the application to cinema of the methods of this school. It too is a form of theatre: not of the academic theatre but of the 'theatre of October'.

Anyone who wants to appreciate the significance of *Potemkin* and to understand the sources it derived from should not forget that Eisenstein was a pupil of Meyerhold. ...

In Eisenstein's film it is objects rather than actors that act. That is why it is not theatre, say the academicians of the theatre. But is it not true that objects act in the theatre of Meyerhold? Was he not the first person to teach us to understand the 'play of objects' and to show us their effective force? ... You can already see all this as a method in Meyerhold's productions of 1922–3. To the enemies of left art this was a 'stunt' but for us it was an assertion of the *new method* of theatrical work that is now, having been translated into cinema, celebrating its triumph.

In *Potemkin* there is no individual hero as there was in the old theatre. It is the mass that acts: the battleship and its sailors and the city and its population in revolutionary mood. Both are organized with great mastery and merged into a complex composition. But the elements of this composition have already been seen in the revolutionary productions of the amateur theatre and in its professional artistic version.... In the methods of revolutionary theatre we have already witnessed a struggle not between individuals, but between classes.... This is the beginning of the path to further theatrical achievements and this is where cinema too derives its strength, as *Potemkin* clearly confirms.

Gvozdev's ulterior motive – the proclamation of revolutionary theatre and its methods as the only legitimate future for Soviet theatre – is perhaps made clear in the final paragraph of his review:

It goes without saying that in establishing this link with the 'Theatrical October' we are not exhausting the characteristics of this remarkable film, which must be viewed independently of theatre as a brilliant and very stylish cinema epic. But this is not the place for that. In the meantime we must resolutely declare that the triumph of *Potemkin* necessitates a re-examination of all the positions that are hostile to the 'Theatrical October', that it raises doubts about the course towards right-wing art that has been taken recently and reminds us forcefully of the need to move from a rejection to an affirmation and a deepening of October in our whole artistic policy.

On 18 June 1925 the Communist Party Politburo had issued a decree entitled 'On the Policy of the Party in the Field of Literature' which was intended to set the framework for Party policy in all the arts, including theatre and cinema. This decree had urged that:

The Party must underline the necessity for the creation of a literature aimed at a genuinely mass readership of workers and peasants.
We must break more boldly and decisively with the traditions of literature for the gentry and make use of all the technical achievements of the old masters to work out an appropriate form,
intelligible *to the millions*.[27]

In the three years that followed this decree a series of conferences
devoted to each art form was held under the auspices of the
Party's Agitprop Department. The conference on cinema was the
last to be held – in March 1928,[28] while the conference on theatre
was held in May 1927. The debates that the decree unleashed,
against a background of growing political and economic centraliza-
tion, often reflected a growing desperation about the present and a
fearful concern for the future. This coloured the cut-and-thrust of
discussion in all Soviet art forms from the mid-1920s, through the
denunciations of the proletarian cultural campaigns of the First
Five-Year Plan of 1928–32, until the whole process culminated in
the decree of 23 April 1932 'On the Reorganization [*perestroika*!] of
Literary and Artistic Organizations',[29] which led on to the promul-
gation of Socialist Realism as the only acceptable framework for
Soviet art in 1934.[30] In his *Zhizn iskusstva* review therefore
Gvozdev was using the critical success of *Potemkin* as a means of
strengthening the case for the kind of *theatre* that he believed in. It
thus served his purpose to demonstrate the continuity that undoubtedly did exist between Eisenstein's film and Meyerhold's theatrical
methods, which Gvozdev was both a leading expert on, and a
leading proponent of.

As far as Eisenstein himself was concerned, the most important
reactions were probably those from his fellow film-makers. These
were largely expressed through the organization known at that time
as ARK, the Association of Revolutionary Cinematography. In its
later incarnation as ARRK, the Association of Workers of Revolutionary Cinema, it was to play the leading role in cinema in
promoting the proletarian cultural revolution that was supposed to
accompany the economic, social and political changes of the first
Five-Year Plan, 1928–32 that culminated in the centralizing decree
of 23 April 1932. But in 1925–6 ARK was still an association – a
kind of trade union for film-makers – that continued to encompass
directors as fundamentally different as Eisenstein and Dziga Vertov,

an organization that had no ideology of its own but rather represented a particular professional interest group. For new films ARK
organized regular Thursday evening viewing sessions followed by
public discussions. These became known as 'ARK Thursdays'.
Sometimes the discussions found their way into the public prints,
sometimes not.

In the case of *The Battleship Potemkin* the first attempt to organize a
joint viewing session for both *Potemkin* and Viskovsky's *The Ninth of
January* on 30 December 1925 proved to be something of a fiasco, as
'One Who Suffered' reported anonymously in the Moscow evening
paper, *Vecherniaia Moskva*:

ARK arranged its usual screening and discussion session yesterday.
There were two films in the programme: *The Ninth of January* and
The Battleship Potemkin.

On this occasion the usually peaceful and somewhat tedious
ARK evening turned into a noisy and very animated 'mass action'
of a scandalous character.

The majority of those *invited* assembled at eight o'clock, when the
second picture was due to begin (an Eisenstein production is of
interest to wide circles). The number of those *invited* far exceeded
the capacity of the premises of the Central House of Art Workers,
where the screenings usually take place.

The auditorium was already full *from the first picture*. There was no
room for the two hundred (and possibly more) people invited, who
had appeared for the start of the *second* picture. Those who had been
invited felt that they had been made fools of and became agitated.
Noise. Shouting. A crush. A scandal develops.

The organizers of the evening find a way out of the situation.
They announce that *The Battleship Potemkin* cannot be shown 'for
technical reasons'. They ask people to disperse. The passive and
trusting people leave. The active and distrustful people make a noise
... and stay behind.

The auditorium becomes jam-packed with people. They wait. The
lights go down and on the screen the long-awaited main title
appears. The incident appears to be closed. Everything is forgotten.

But ... the lights blaze up again, the 'organizer' goes up on stage
and announces: '*Potemkin* cannot be shown ... We have a bad copy
... It is already very late...'

At this point those who had been *invited* roared out. The audience thunders, seethes with indignation, shouts in unison. It no longer listens to the 'organizers' who are trying to say something. It is demanding satisfaction.

This 'mass action' reaches a peak of tension and lasts a very long time. The hour approaches eleven o'clock.

When passions subside, the 'Protestants' gradually disperse.[31]

A subsequent attempt was obviously successful, because the discussion of *Potemkin* under the auspices of ARK did take place on one of their regular 'Thursday evenings' on 7 January 1926.[32] ARK also circulated a questionnaire to its members about the film. The results were published in the February 1926 issue of the association's house journal *Kinozhurnal ARK*, but would have been known to Eisenstein and others before publication.[33] Reactions were not as uniformly enthusiastic as the early reviews had been. The critic Khrisanf Khersonsky, describing Eisenstein as 'a grown-up engineer' and praising the montage of attractions as a proven method, made the remark that was to dog Eisenstein's work throughout his career: '*Potemkin* is made with a fine head but inside it is somehow cold.' Khersonsky also endorsed the accessibility of Eisenstein's latest film:

The director does not stew in the emotional stomach juices of his own feelings; he does not wander around in a mist of 'inspirations' and timid conjectures. The director does not want to work in the dark, not seeing his audience. He turns his face towards the audience. He makes a film for the audience. The director works in a socially useful fashion and contrives his missile – his film – so that it can be fired at the masses, just as an engineer calculatingly refines the technology of an object according to a precise plan. What before Eisenstein was done in an amateurish, groping and intuitive manner, Eisenstein does strictly consciously.[34]

Vsevolod Pudovkin, director of another anniversary film, based on Maxim Gorky's *The Mother*, was equally enthusiastic, but expressed some reservations:

First of all, this is beautiful cinema. The whole of the raw material is given depth on an exclusively cinematic level. The intertitles, which are an organic part of the whole work, are broken down into separate words for the first time and serve as rhythmic elements.

The montage forcibly directs the spectator. Eisenstein masters it brilliantly and leads the spectator almost into pathos.

The work of the cameraman demonstrates boldness and close contact with the director. As for those who perform the individual roles, they are all bad, except for the almost static moments involving non-actors. This is partly the fault of the director, who has not mastered his human material. Almost all the work done by these people is depressingly banal. (The villain has a crooked smile, the hero knots his brow and stares.) The few weaknesses that I have mentioned do not mean that this is not a work of great significance or that the individual montage and shot constructions (which are undoubtedly innovative) are not brilliantly executed. On the whole this is high-tension cinema, powerfully impressive.

Olga Rakhmanova, who had co-directed *Behind White Lines* from Nina Agadzhanova's first script the previous year, echoed Pudovkin's comments:

> The screenplay is fine. It reflects our epoch and provides clear and literate intertitles that are interesting in both their style and content. The work of the director is bold and interesting and demonstrates huge originality and inventiveness, great artistic taste and knowledge of the spectator as a human being.

> The work of the cameraman shows talent. But I do not like some of the performers in close up: the student agitating by the coffin, the mother of the baby in the pram and the particularly uninteresting and contrived priest.[35]

Pudovkin's criticism of the results that Eisenstein had achieved from his actors reflects the difference in attitude between the two directors towards the role of the individual actor in cinema. The differing role of the actor on stage and screen was one of the crucial issues in contemporary Soviet debates about the distinctions between theatre and cinema, and thus also a defining factor in determining the specificity of cinema. Indeed in the last issue of *Kinozhurnal ARK* for 1925 Khrisanf Khersonsky had gone so far as to argue:

> There are not yet any cinema actors in the USSR. And at the same time there are a very great number. From these 'many' we must find

the few and create real screen people ... Cinema is not content with
the transfer of actors from the stage, the circus or the vaudeville ...
The man of the screen is the new man.[36]

But there were further disagreements about the proper role of the actor
on screen and here there were crucial differences between Eisenstein on
the one hand and Kuleshov and his pupil Pudovkin on the other. These
differences immediately become clear if we compare the different
functions that the actors perform in *Potemkin* and *The Mother.* Pudovkin
uses individual named actors and their individual emotions to represent
the emotions of the mass through individual characters who are
demonstrably human beings. Eisenstein uses his human material
(trained or untrained and at this stage largely unnamed and unknown)
in a symbolic, somewhat dehumanized manner reminiscent, superfi-
cially at least, of Meyerhold's biomechanical actor or Kuleshov's
'model actor' or *naturshchik.* But this comparison is only a superficial
one: the actors in both Meyerhold's theatre and Kuleshov's cinema had
been highly trained to produce maximum emotional effect with
minimal physical gesture. Eisenstein's 'actors' were chosen in accordance with the principles of 'typage', because they quite simply looked
the part.

Nonetheless, it might at first appear rather surprising that
Kuleshov refused to be drawn by the questionnaire into saying
anything of any great significance about *Potemkin,* but confined his
remarks to the rather grudging: 'On the questions of the script and
the director, I abstain. The work of the cameraman is extremely
satisfactory.' This was hardly an enthusiastic endorsement, but it may
have been quite simply that Kuleshov was still smarting from Eisenstein's rejection of his notion of serial montage in favour of his own
advocacy of the montage of attractions. In 1924 in 'The Montage of
Film Attractions' Eisenstein had defined his position as follows: 'The
method of the montage of attractions is the comparison of subjects
for thematic effect.'[37] For him the effectiveness of montage depended
not, as it did for Kuleshov, on *sequence* but, in effect, on *interrupted
sequence* or *conflict.* The comparisons were developed in Eisenstein's
'Beyond the Shot',[38] published in 1929, but the difference of opinion
was already known and felt three years earlier at the time of *Potemkin's* release.

The harshest criticism to appear in *Kinozhurnal ARK* came however
from Alexei Gan, a Constructivist artist and ardent supporter of Dziga

Vertov's Cine-Eye school of documentary film-making to which Eisenstein was fundamentally opposed. Gan was even more grudging than Kuleshov in his compliments, but damning in his criticisms:

> The script is written for an anniversary. It is an eclectic work on the strictly aesthetic level. The work of the cameraman is good, but sentimental. The individual performers illustrate well the eclectic method of the production. *Potemkin* sows confusion in Soviet cinema. As a whole, it is a bad picture.

The reactions to this questionnaire set the framework for the Thursday evening discussion held under the auspices of ARK in January 1926. As was normal ARK practice, the film-makers had the first and last word. Eduard Tisse, the cameraman on *Potemkin*, opened the proceedings and the final remarks were left to Eisenstein.

Tisse was concerned to do two things in his introductory remarks. The first was to nail the rumour that the film had taken eighteen months to make: the shooting and editing had in fact taken only two and a half months, from September to December. The second was to explain some of the technical problems that had to be overcome to produce what we should nowadays call the special effects:

> We began the shooting in Odessa. The most important scenes there were those around the steps. Very many of the shots entailed technical difficulties – for instance, the shots of the pram. For this we had to make an entire construction of rails along which the pram moved downwards. There were occasions when we had to film rapid movement, for example as the pram descended, and our assistants could not hold the rope because their hands were burning, so we had to place other people below to catch the pram. Other stunts, such as the scene where the child is trampled underfoot by the fleeing crowd, were filmed as follows. We took an ordinary beam and two workers held it between them. The people fleeing ran across this beam, which carried them over the child, so that they only touched him lightly with their feet. In this way the child did not, of course, suffer at all.

Tisse was also, perhaps not surprisingly, concerned to point out to his audience that the morning, evening and night effects were all achieved by the camera rather than by hand-tinting:

21. Filming the Odessa Steps sequence: how to trample a child without hurting him. Eisenstein is squatting on the steps, with Tisse behind the camera

My aim on the whole was to manage to communicate the director's intentions using all sorts of devices. For example, to communicate the morning, all the night and morning effects, and the transition to evening. Here Sergei Mikhailovich and I had to combine our resources. We had, for instance, to communicate the transition to night etc., not by tinting the film, but through the shooting, i.e. we had to communicate it optically on screen.... Here we were moving away from the previous practice of tinting, and trying to communicate night through normal filming.

He concluded, to applause, by emphasizing how much hard work had gone into the making of the film in such a short space of time before the anniversary for which it had been commissioned: 'We worked, as I have already said, between sixteen and eighteen hours a day and it was only because of this that we were able to make and finish what has been shown to you.'

The next speaker was the director Leo Moor [Mur] who, with Abram Room and others, was making another anniversary film *Krasnaia Presnia*, about the Moscow workers' uprising in that part of the city in October 1905, based on another script by Nina Agadzha-nova-Shutko.[39] While supporting the montage of attractions as an effective method of film-making, Moor was critical of the name that Eisenstein had given this method:

> The basic method used by Eisenstein is one that he calls the montage of attractions. This name is not quite correct. Eisenstein is arranging [*montiruet*] not just the film, but also the spectator's brain cells. This is not montage of attractions but of associations. The montage is not just on the cinema screen but also on the screen of the brain. The method acts upon the spectator's emotional impressionability [*vpe-chatliaemost*] and achieves the results required. Of course the insistence on the montage of associations sometimes involves a certain stiffness (the association between the simmering borshch and the crowd is, for instance, strained), the association between the hand stroking the cross and that stroking the dagger is strained, but I think that the method itself is absolutely correct and worth imitating.[40]

Speaking from his own experience in Hollywood, Moor identified the roots of Eisenstein's montage techniques as being with Griffith:

> This method was not born from Eisenstein's head in the way that Athene Pallas was born from Jupiter's. The montage of association method has been applied to a whole series of American pictures. Eisenstein has refined this method with skill and brilliance.

Moor then turned to the question of mass action and the role of the hero in *The Battleship Potemkin*:

> It is worth saying a few words about mass action and the absence of heroes. There are individual heroes in the film but they are not given names. It seems to me that it is quite impossible to convey mass action as such. It will always be broken down into its individual constituent parts. A long shot of a mass scene is always like unpressed caviar.
> Eisenstein unearths a whole series of individual elements from the mass and, by using close-ups, he conveys the impression of the mass. This is an ingenious device. Eisenstein is a master of detailed work: he is a jeweller rather than a blacksmith. The 'mass' method is not, of course, the only one. Although the masses create history,

not all life's phenomena can be treated as mass action. There is, for instance, no way in which a declaration of love can be constructed on the basis of mass scenes. The most important thing is not the mass method, but the method of the montage of associations.

Moor congratulated Eisenstein on the refinement of the methods that he had used in his first feature film *The Strike*:

> In *The Strike* Eisenstein was more original but there was no synthetic montage in that film. In *The Strike* each scene was worked out analytically but when put together they did not create the required effect. In *Potemkin*, apart from the analytical montage, there is also synthetic montage. The spectator assembles the scenes in his own brain just as Eisenstein wanted him to do.
>
> Everything depends on how successful the individual details are and on how well they are put together. In the work that we have seen on the screen you can sense a fine cinematic approach. Eisenstein is a man of great cunning: he knows how to select raw material that will speak for itself. The battleship is that kind of raw material: it does not have to be beautified or touched up with actors. All honour and glory to Eisenstein for the fact that, even though he has only very recently come to us from the theatre, he realized straight away the principles by which photogenic raw material is selected. He knows how to chew over this material so that there is nothing left for other directors to do with it.

In his original speech Moor singled out Eduard Tisse for particular praise, but the remarks that follow were excised from the version published at the time:

> I want to remark on the moments of collective creativity in the work of Eisenstein's group. ... I am not, of course, saying that he should not lay claim to the laurels, but his work was only possible with the support of a collective that was strong and joined together in a tight organization. These were his assistants, and above all his cameraman Tisse. I am afraid to say this, but he ought perhaps to be placed even higher than Eisenstein is. A number of shots reach the spectator only because they were beautifully shot by the cameraman. Eisenstein depicts the mists beautifully. These mists are one of the elements that provoke the required feeling, the required emotion in

the spectator because of the way that they have been shot. If there had been a different cameraman incapable of producing these shots a number of effects would have been lost to us.[41]

The next speaker was the critic Ippolit Sokolov, whose comments were not published at the time. In 1934 Sokolov was to produce a literary script of *Potemkin*, based on the release print, and in January 1926 he was largely fulsome in his praise, even if approaching the film from a very different perspective from that of Moor:

> I think that history will regard *The Battleship Potemkin* as the third [key] date in the history of Soviet cinema. The first date was of course *The Little Red Devils* [Krasnye d''iavoliata, dir: Ivan Per-estiani, 1923], the second historic date was *The Strike* and the third is *The Battleship Potemkin*. All the other films were just raw material to fill in the gaps between these three dates. Above all this is a film on the level of really great art, which has not perhaps yet been seen in Soviet cinema. It is the kind of work of art that people will think, write and talk about seriously for a very long time, just as we suppose that they will think, write and talk about Mayakovsky's poetry, Meyerhold's stage productions and the constructions of Rod-chenko and others in the art of the October Revolution. Above all Eisenstein feels and creates his own particular style, which may really be called the style of our epoch. This Constructivist style is asserted in both the raw material and the form of the director's and cameraman's treatment in the picture. What is most striking in the picture is the unity and consistency from the very first shot to the very last – be it the sea, the battleship, or simply the *mise-en-scène* – in accordance with the real unity of Constructivist style. Eisenstein's raw material has turned out to be photogenic. The sea and the sky are always most photogenic and Eisenstein, being a great artist, has a sense for this genuinely photographic material.[42]

While agreeing with Moor's critique of the 'montage of attractions', Sokolov disagreed, however, with his assessment of the strengths of that montage in *Potemkin*:

> If I pass immediately to the characteristics of the picture's con-struction I can only say that in my view Eisenstein is a much worse theorist than he is an artist. This montage that people are

already beginning to praise him for – this terribly unfortunate expression and unhappy notion of the 'attraction' – is all quite uncharacteristic of him. In the final analysis this picture succeeds not by dint of the details but because of the long shot.[43] In this picture the best thing is the long shot of the battleship while some of the details are not always entirely satisfactory. For example, the pram and the individual moments of the shooting of the crowd on the steps are not entirely successful because they have been exaggerated by close-ups.

This striving for detail does not correspond to Eisenstein's style or to the style that is reflected in the film as a whole. The unity of the Constructivist style requires a large-scale use of the long shot, rather than the [devices] of the decadent American and German cinematic era. To praise Eisenstein for using close-ups even in mass scenes is, in my view, to miss the point of the picture, to miss its unity, to miss its style.

Sokolov was followed by the film director Abram Room, co-director with Leo Moor of *Krasnaia Presnia*. Room was the first person to place *Potemkin* between fiction and documentary film and also one of the first (alongside Khrisanf Khersonsky) to make the subsequently common criticism that there was an absence of humanity in Eisenstein's work:[44]

The method that Eisenstein uses in making pictures like *The Strike* and *Potemkin*, i.e. pictures on a historic scale, is undoubtedly a good one that produces a real and necessary effect. If we analyse the chemical composition of this method we shall find that it consists of two elements: one is the 'Cine-Eye', while the other is so-called fiction film (*khudozhestvennaia kinematografiia*). The amalgam, the formula for which is known to Eisenstein, produces a very real effect, it produces a clot, and it puts a number of events in perspective. But the characteristic feature of this method is its antipathy towards humanity.

The 'Potemkin' and all the material, the objects on it, are depicted by the director exactly as they exist in real life, but when he turns to people there is a great discrepancy. We see that there are no people.

The people are handled in a schematic fashion reminiscent of machines.

The whole time we see the prow of the ship and machinery – and this leaves us cold. When Vakulinchuk dies, a significant part of the power of the film goes with him. There are five or so officers depicted in *Potemkin* and you get confused because you do not recognize them. When they are thrown overboard you think that it is the same person being thrown overboard again and again. None of them has a face.

The story of the steps does not move us. The title is done artistically: 'Don't shoot! My boy is hurt!', but the actress gives a dry and cold performance. The spectator demands: give us a human being...[45]

In the unpublished version of his speech Room went on:

When we see raw material conveyed in its natural form it produces an effect but the person working on it makes no impression. In my view this is a large minus in a very useful work.

I do not think that this passion for collective heroes and mass scenes can continue for long. I have to say that nobody has done mass scenes better than Kuleshov. In *The Death Ray* [Luch smerti, released 16 April 1925], for instance, the mass scenes were definitely interesting and well done and in this sense the various mass scenes in *Potemkin* repeat some parts of that film. Kuleshov set the standard for the mass scene and it will provoke a whole series of imitations. But, even when we have such good examples, we cannot stick to mass scenes for long. We shall have to move from close-ups of mass scenes to close-ups of individual people, of an individual person.[46]

Room concluded with the optimistic assertion that: 'A human being stands at the centre of a whole number of distinguished films and I am certain that, if Eisenstein makes another four *Potemkins*, in the fifth he will come back to a human being.'[47]

Room was followed by the relatively unknown scriptwriter and director Alexander Dubrovsky. He said initially that, as a scriptwriter himself, he would confine his remarks to the script, but in fact he concentrated on the content of the film. Given that Eisenstein had departed very considerably from Nuné's original script for *The Year 1905*, this is perhaps scarcely surprising. A short extract from his comments was published in *Kinozhurnal ARK* at the time, but what he had to say is worth reproducing at greater length here:

The Battleship Potemkin is such a great work of cinema that it would be pointless to talk about it as a whole. For this reason I should like to draw your attention to one aspect of the work: i.e. its content. I think it is extremely important because, from what we know of the worker audience, they tend to assess any work from the point of view of its content. In this respect *The Battleship Potemkin* has both great merits and a number of weaknesses. There can be no doubt that Eisenstein's great victory lies in his depiction of collective action.... He has demonstrated that pictures that have the collective as their hero concede nothing in terms of their success or interest to films with individual heroes.

But in this script, in the content of this work, there is a great defect, above all in terms of its scope. Here in five parts we have essentially the first part of *The Strike*, here divided into five parts. Here we are shown the first moment of the 'strike' on the battleship, namely the mutiny. We know that [in real life] this was followed by a mutiny aboard the 'St George the Victor', by the 'Potemkin's' departure for Romania, its defeat and return. None of this is shown. The social scope is also not great: we see nothing apart from the 'Potemkin' and the script exaggerates this one event to excess. The film depicts too small and isolated a group of events. In this respect, perhaps, the content will be somewhat monotonous to the innocent eye. In any event at a second viewing this picture already seems rather tedious because the moments that grabbed you the first time round no longer do because you have already lost interest in the content itself.

As for the actual content of the film, it suffers from considerable defects. However we must not forget that this is a historical picture: it should depict the events of 1905 and we know from history that the mutiny on the battleship 'Potemkin' was a fact. But here we have both what actually happened and what has been invented, and invented very feebly. Let us take as an example the scene on the eve of the mutiny. The sailors are lying in hammocks of some kind, flexing their muscles and even holding meetings in these very hammocks. This scene is utterly unconvincing.

Now let us take the actual moment of the mutiny. In actual fact the mutiny occurred because of the *borshch*.[48] The sailor Vaku-linchuk had a sharp exchange with the First Officer and the officer shot him with his revolver. This sailor was murdered. In the film an entirely new sequence of events has been devised. The First

Officer kills the sailor after the ship has been seized by the muti-neers. At the same time as the majority of the officers are being thrown overboard, we see this officer chasing Vakulinchuk across the deck and shooting him. This is not entirely convincing. Then there is the next stunt with the tarpaulin. I do not recall this moment from history. This case seems unconvincing because in 1905 there were indeed mass executions and mass shootings but they were carried out by a court. The scene in which twenty or so sailors are covered [with a tarpaulin] and shot on the spot without trial, on the orders of the captain alone, cries out against historical truth. This could only have occurred aboard a pirate ship in an adventure film.[49]

In reality the demonstrators were shot after the battleship had left: the participants were shot when there was nobody to help the workers. The film depicts the battleship remaining in Odessa. Look at the combination that Eisenstein depicts: the ship and the steps are so close that they almost greet one another, and it is on these very steps that the shooting begins, while the sailors, seeing what is happening, do not intervene. This also produces an unconvincing impression.

Then there are the boats: they provoke a smile when we see how, on the director's orders, the mass of boats simultaneously raise their masts and sails and approach the battleship and then in precisely the same way, at his command, they lower their sails and some old woman boards the ship carrying a goose, and so on. These are the basic facts from the content of the film, which will provoke doubts about their authenticity and will be unintelligible to the simpler audience. Generally speaking this picture leaves a great deal to be desired in terms of its content and is not at all satisfactory. It encompasses a fragment of the year 1905 and does not show the connection between the mutiny and the other revolutionary events. It is just a particular episode.[50]

Dubrovsky's comments on *Potemkin* were the last from this discussion to be published in the February 1926 issue of *Kinozhurnal ARK*. But the minutes of the meeting show that there were contributions from two other speakers before Eisenstein himself was given the final word. Dubrovsky was followed by the distinguished Formalist critic, script-writer, author and later Eisenstein biographer, Viktor Shklovsky, who also published a separate review of the film in the same issue of the journal, entitled quite simply 'Eisenstein'.[51] In his speech Shklovsky began by defending Eisenstein against Dubrovsky's criticisms:

Comrades, the previous speaker reminded me of a meeting of some screenplay committee with its carping criticisms. I am not an unqualified advocate of Eisenstein but there is a difference between what Eisenstein has done – and he has done a lot and done it well – and what others do. The difference is not an ideological one, but a difference between a great and talented man and people who do not understand what it is that they want to do.[52]

He went on to defend Eisenstein against the charge that *Potemkin* was historically inauthentic:

Seeing the really untalented *The Ninth of January* and the brilliant *Potemkin* people emerge as if they have just read a book badly. They ask, 'Why didn't you film the whole year 1905 and the Russo-Japanese War?' Eisenstein's talent lies in his ability to organize a film [about the year 1905] even though he only filmed in Odessa, Sebastopol and on the 'Potemkin'. You have to know how to break loose from your client because, if you fulfil all his demands, you will make a bad film.... I think that the historical authenticity is of the kind that you would find only in a historical picture.

In his published review, however, Shklovsky reiterated the view expressed by others that Eisenstein was bad at handling individual human characters. After praising the Odessa Steps sequence as 'worth all the Russian scripts that have preceded it', he went on, 'The best scenes in the film are those in which there are no people working. That means the fifth part, which is composed of guns and battleships.'[53] Shklovsky offered an explanation for Eisenstein's use of close-ups, criticized by Sokolov and praised by Moor:

While not in full control of human movement and handling mass scenes primitively but also extremely ingeniously, Eisenstein is capable of brilliantly handling human immobility, people standing in mourning, and this forces him to create his mass scenes from extreme close-ups.

The review closed with high praise for the cameraman Eduard Tisse: 'The camera work is not felt as something separate, but is logically connected to the whole semantic structure of the film. This is the greatest praise that can be given to the cameraman alone. Tisse films like a man should breathe.'

The last contributor before Eisenstein's closing remarks was the cameraman Mikhail Gindin.[54] Returning to the question of the historical authenticity of *Potemkin*, he recalled the impact of the film's screening and in particular the very real effect that it had had on those who had participated in the events depicted, however symbolically, indirectly or 'inaccurately' on screen:

> I want to dwell on only one matter and that concerns the success of this film among the general public. Many people have mentioned its technical and directorial merits but I want to bring one fact to your attention. When this film was shown in the Bolshoi Theatre at a congress of former political prisoners, who had come from all over Russia and also included those who had participated in the events of 1905, I could not sit through the fifth and final part because there was such sound and noise, such emotion, such a sense of experiencing reality that it just made you tremble. Everyone who was watching the film experienced something definite at that moment. Some of those sitting near me – possibly participants in the mutiny – began to shed tears, despite the fact that they were Old Bolshevik workers. This is proof of the fact that the picture will be successful. . . .[55]

The closing speech was made by Eisenstein. Before speaking, however, he demanded that Alexei Gan, the only person to have described *Potemkin* as 'bad', justify his comments before the ARK audience. Not surprisingly, Gan declined, but the animosity between a supporter of the Cine-Eyes and the director who had been accused of using their methods, was crystal clear. Eisenstein's remarks to the ARK discussion group included his reactions to the reservations and criticisms expressed by his fellow film-makers and thus help us to understand *Potemkin* more clearly. Many of his other thoughts on the film have been translated into English elsewhere but these have not. For this reason I think that it would be useful to reproduce them here in full:

> The fact is that in the final analysis I do not have to say anything and for this Comrade Gan is responsible. It would have been interesting for me to find out more about his attacks. I could examine them in detail, point by point as I noted them down, but that would

hardly be much fun. Until Shklovsky spoke it would have been possible to count on something, but now there is very little left to say.

Now I shall respond to the speeches. Nobody approached this work in the way that they usually approach a discussion of something. Nobody posed the question: why was this film made? Comrade Gan should be ashamed that he did not put this question forward: that seems to be his speciality. When you analyse an item of furniture, a kiosk for selling literature etc., you ask is the literature well displayed, is the kiosk comfortable for the salesperson to sit in, and so on. I think that the task of this picture was a very special one. The task of a film about 1905 is grounded in an upbeat mood, not a mournful one, because our assessment of all the events of that year is definitely in the major key. When I brought this material to Moscow and asked when the film was going to be released, I was told that it might never be fully released, but that it was going to be shown in the Bolshoi Theatre. It is from this perspective that the picture should be judged. I was very pleased to hear from the comrade whose name I do not know [i.e. Mikhail Gindin – RT] that the effect that I wanted was achieved during the screening for former political prisoners.

I was particularly amused by Comrade Room's speech but first of all I want to say something about Comrade Dubrovsky. Comrade Shklovsky said that I had very skilfully and cunningly cut out this picture and this material from the bare essentials. Anyone who is familiar with the history of the 'Potemkin' knows very well what actually happened. When Comrade Dubrovsky asks why there's no scene showing the 'St George the Victor' joining the mutiny etc., I can only add that the ship ran aground. Next question: why didn't we show it taking on its cargo, and so on. It's just as well that we don't show all this because we can see from *The Ninth of January* how people were shot in nine different districts in the same way that people tear coupons out of a ration book. If Dubrovsky is saying that he only found the film interesting when he watched it for the first time, whereas the second time he found it boring, there is only one thing that I can say in reply: go and see *The Ninth of January*. Furthermore, you do not have to go and see a film twenty-five times: it was no part of my task [to cater for that].

As for Comrade Room I have to put the question like this. When I was listening to him I got the impression that the film made absolutely no impression and Comrade Room, being a decent man, was explaining why the film makes no impression. He went on to say that, if you cut out the intertitles, even the fifth part would not make any impression. I ask then: why cut out these titles, if their presence produces an effect? I shall refrain from commenting on the actual question of the intertitles and the acting because I think that it will be more interesting to discuss these once we have seen *The Bay of Death*.[56] (*Comrade Khersonsky from the floor: 'You shouldn t talk about a film that hasn t been released.'*) I've seen it already and I can tell you that in the final reel during the fighting Room has a more startling intertitle that should not be released [i.e. omitted – RT] under any circumstances. The sailors are running around and then we see the title 'Panic': and I think that, if we remove the title, there will be no panic. As for my titles, I think that I have here observed the very correct device of economy: why force people to open their eyes wide and breathe more heavily to produce the impression that the squadron is advancing if I can produce a title that will do the job? This is far from being such a bad thing to do.

What is more, when we view *The Bay of Death* I shall insist on speaking about the acting of one particular person who seems to substitute for everything that I have in the titles. To Comrade Moor I have to say that there is in my film a mass declaration of love – between the skiffs and the battleship. One more curious thing. It is, as it were, a tributary of the original mainstream that people have been telling me about here: that in *Potemkin* there is a noticeable departure from my previous work and from *The Strike*, that the new film is made differently, that I have compromised, and so on. I think it is more important, however, that in this case the work moves people and makes an impression, and, when all is said and done, that there is no repetition of what happened with *The Strike*. Despite the fact that the film was praised at the start it has done very badly in the cinemas. In time I shall learn to combine what I want to do with the spectator's demands, but for the time being I shall permit myself to depart from my previous work so that this film is more attuned to the public taste. I believe that this is the right way to address the question.

Then one comrade said that the long shots were not well done. I have to say that in the course of the whole picture there is not a single long shot of the 'Potemkin' and this is for the simple reason that the 'Potemkin' does not exist, because we had to sew it together piece by piece.

As far as historical accuracy is concerned, I must make one personal observation. The old woman with the goose was not there in
1905 because she is my own mother and I know that she wasn't
there. . . . I do not know what else to say to you, so let me end on
this note.[57]

For Eisenstein this was the conclusion only as far as the ARK discussion was concerned. His many other comments on *Potemkin* from 1926
onwards are indicated in the relevant section of the further reading at
the end of this book.

The ARK 'Thursday evening' was, of course, also far from being the
conclusion of critical reaction to the film in either Moscow or the
Soviet Union as a whole. It is however interesting to note that the gist
of most of the subsequent comments on the film are to be found, albeit
sometimes in very embryonic form, in the speeches made to this
meeting, which is why I have reproduced them at such length. The
issue of *Kinozhurnal ARK* that carried the reports of the ARK
'Thursday evening' also included a review by its editor, Nikolai
Lebedev, one of the founders of ARK, under the heading 'The Six
Arguments of *Potemkin*', which can be summarized as follows:

1 *Potemkin* . . . has shown that *our film technology has reached that of
   the West in terms of production quality.* But we are still poor. . .
2 Eisenstein's *Potemkin* has shown that *the formal heights of the old*
   (bourgeois) *cinema have not only been quickly achieved* but may also
   be surpassed. . .
3 In the narrow debate about whether a film should have a hero
   Eisenstein's *Potemkin* has proved that the *'heroless film has at least
   as much right to exist as any other well-made drama*. . .
4 In the 'great debate' about the Soviet film repertoire, about the
   revolution and classicism, 'contemporary' and 'historical' subject-
   matter *Potemkin* . . . has proved that *the prospect of victory is moving
   ever more clearly and definitely towards the former*. . .
5 *Potemkin*, made by the commercial enterprise Goskino, has
   proved that, in evaluating *the social (and economic) significance of
   works of art it is not always necessary to compete in the market place*. . .
6 *Potemkin*, a work of cinema, has proved that cinema is the most
   powerful art form of our age. *Potemkin* has convinced and subdued
   those who quite recently were conservatives and cinephobes. . . .
   After this picture you can scarcely find any 'country bumpkins'

who are prepared to risk denying the power of cinema. Neither theatre, nor fine art, nor literature has given the Revolution works that can equate in expression to this work of cinema.

Henceforth there can be no doubt that for today cinema is the pioneer and leader of the arts.[58]

It is small wonder that the editorial for that same issue, also written by Nikolai Lebedev, hailed *Potemkin* as a 'huge victory'. Describing the articles in the February 1926 issue of *Kinozhurnal ARK* as 'more lyricism than analysis', he went on:

But tomorrow, the day after tomorrow and for a long time afterwards film-makers will study this magnificent film through a magnifying glass, classify its methods, learn from it, and use it to teach the young generation in our film schools.[59]

Despite the largely enthusiastic reception ⸮among critics and film-makers in the Soviet capital Moscow, it was in the end *Potemkin*'s reception in the German capital Berlin that made its international reputation as a film that, while it might be suppressed, censored and cut, could by no means be ignored.

Potemkin was first shown in Berlin as early as 21 January 1926, three days after its Moscow release, at a closed memorial meeting for Lenin, who had died two years previously, in the Großes Schauspielhaus, a neo-classical building originally designed by Adolf Schinkel and one of the largest performance spaces in the city.[60] The audience was composed of workers and intellectuals on the political left. The occasion was organized by Willi Münzenberg, the leading German Communist organizer and propagandist.[61] He had already put Workers' International Relief funds into what had consequently become the Mezhrabpom-Rus film studio in Moscow. Now, after discovering that the Lloyd firm had signed a contract to import 25 Soviet films into Germany but that the firm had turned down *Potemkin*, Münzenberg set up another company, Prometheus-Film specifically to contract from the Soviet cinema authorities the German distribution rights for Eisenstein's film. As a workers' publisher, producer and propagandist, Münzenberg certainly knew what he was doing and how to go about doing it. There were several factors that explain *Potemkin*'s success in Germany. One of these was undoubtedly Münzenberg's understanding of his audience, but the strength of support for the

Communist Party in Germany at that time and associated sympathies with the Soviet Union as a new and better civilization played their part. The prolonged and increasingly desperate efforts by military and right-wing circles to ban the film enabled Münzenberg to organize a protest against these efforts under the banner of freedom of speech, thus gaining support from liberal elements in the population. Last but not least, the unforgettable score by Edmund Meisel that accompanied the public showings of the film made an enormous impact on those who experienced it.

In March 1926 Prometheus, as was required by law, submitted a copy of the film to the Berlin film censors' office, which took rather longer than was usual to come to a decision because of an intervention from the War Ministry. Two senior officials from the Ministry, including the Army (Reichswehr) Chief of Staff, General Hans von Seeckt, who had in 1920 declined to call out the army to put down an attempted putsch against the new Weimar Republic, uttering the deadly phrase 'Reichswehr does not fire upon Reichswehr',[62] were given a secret preview of *Potemkin* at the Ministry on 17 March.[63] They realized immediately that the film represented a threat to their interests. The Communist Party was already a major political force in Germany and the right was rumoured to be plotting a military coup. The right had never been happy with the relatively relaxed censorship laws of the Weimar Republic: Article 118 of the Weimar Constitution, guaranteeing freedom of speech and of the press, specifically forbade censorship in general, while permitting legal controls over obscenity. This loophole facilitated an attempt later in 1926 to reintroduce more stringent censorship in the guise of a pornography law, which the writer Gerhart Hauptmann described as the biggest threat to intellectual freedom in his lifetime.[64] The new law, restricting access for minors, was eventually passed by the Reichstag on 3 December 1926 but only after the so-called *Tendenzklausel* had been added. This prevented a work of art from being banned 'because of its political, social, religious, ethical or philosophical content', a clear echo of the *Potemkin* case.[65] In the context of these events *Potemkin* became something of a litmus test. On 24 March, in the light of representations from both the War Ministry and the Reich Commissariat for the Supervision of Public Order, the second Berlin censorship office banned *The Battleship Potemkin* on the grounds that 'the film was likely to endanger public order and security on a lasting basis'.[66]

The day after this secret preview, 18 March, Eisenstein and Tisse arrived in Berlin. They were originally supposed to stay for two weeks and their visit had several purposes: to study the organization, working methods and technical equipment of German film studios, and to acquaint themselves with the latest developments in German films.[67] It was not part of the original intention to attend the premiere of *Potemkin* but, as the prospect loomed, they stayed on. In a letter to his mother on 20 March Eisenstein wrote:

> As long as the money holds out we are living 'like aristocrats'. I don't know how things will work out. We'll be back in ten to twelve days. I can't stand it for longer. I want to work. There's nothing wrong with being a *bon viveur* and a *flâneur* – but not *for long*. . . .[68]

During their stay the pair visited the sets of both Fritz Lang's *Metropolis* and F. W. Murnau's *Faust*, where Eisenstein met Emil Jannings, the German actor he most admired. He also met the violinist, conductor and composer Edmund Meisel, whom Gorky's wife Maria Andreyeva (who worked at that time for the Soviet trade delegation in Berlin) had already commissioned to write a score to accompany the German screenings of *Potemkin*. Meisel had composed scores using jazz and 'noise music' (*Geräuschmusik*) for the radical stage productions of Erwin Piscator, which often included film footage. *Potemkin* was his first commission for a feature-film score but not his last.[69] Writing in 1939, Eisenstein recalled:

> My first work on sound film dates from . . . 1926. And it concerned that same *Potemkin*. The fact is that *Potemkin* – in terms of its fate abroad – was one of the very few films furnished with a specially written score: that is, in silent cinema it came extremely close to the way any sound film is arranged.
>
> However, it is not at all a question here of the fact that Edmund Meisel wrote special music for *Potemkin*. Music has been written for other films, both before and after *Potemkin* . . . in our case the important thing is *how* the music for *Potemkin* was written.
>
> It was written in the same way that nowadays we work with a sound track. More accurately, *as one should work* with a sound track, always, in every way and everywhere, with the creative co-operation and friendly co-creation of the composer and the director.
>
> In fact, despite everything, sound film music even now is almost always 'close to the film' and doesn't basically differ from one-time 'musical illustrations'.[70]

22. Eisenstein (right) and Tisse (5th from right) meet Fritz Lang (4th from right) on the set of Long's *Metropolis*, Berlin, March 1926

Here Eisenstein was reading back into his collaboration with Meisel the origins of the view expressed in his 1928 'Statement on Sound', and later developed elsewhere, that 'musical illustrations' were only one possibility for sound cinema, one aspect of the kind of audiovisual counterpoint that was undoubtedly a feature of Meisel's *Potemkin* score:[71]

> However, with *Potemkin* it was different – admittedly not in everything and far from completely. I was not in Berlin long enough while the music was being commissioned (1926). But, nevertheless it was long enough to come to an agreement with the composer Meisel about the decisive 'effect' of the music for *Potemkin*.
>   Especially about the 'music of the machines' in the encounter with the squadron. For this scene I not only categorically demanded that the composer reject *the usual melodic quality* and the emphasis on *the bare rhythmic beat of the percussion*, but, in so doing, essentially *forced the music as well at this decisive juncture to 'jump over' into a 'new quality : into a noise construction.*

At this point *Potemkin* itself explodes stylistically beyond the limits of the genre of a 'silent picture with musical illustration' into a new field – into *sound film*, in which the genuine specimens of this art form live in a unity of fused musical and visual images, *which have thereby created a single audiovisual image for the work.*

It is to precisely these elements, *which anticipate the possibility of the inner essence of the composition of sound film*, that the 'Meeting the Squadron' scene owes its 'shattering' effect, which abroad is equal to that of the 'Odessa Steps' and is cited in all the anthologies.

Meanwhile Prometheus had appealed against the ban, calling Erwin Piscator and the leading critic Alfred Kerr as expert witnesses and, despite the best efforts of their opponents, the appeal went in their favour. On 10 April 1926 the Supreme Film Censor's Office (*Filmoberprüfstelle*) in Berlin decided by a single casting vote to pass the film for adult audiences only, accepting the film company's argument that the earlier decision breached the cinema censorship laws which expressly forbade the censorship of a film 'because of its political, social, religious, ethical or ideological tendencies *as such*'.[72] The censors required 14 cuts totalling 30 metres, including several from the Odessa Steps sequence, the most significant of which was 9.5 metres long – from the shot of the mother keeling over backwards and pushing her baby in the pram down the steps until it overturns to the shot of a Cossack wielding his whip. Given the need for orchestral rehearsals this gave Meisel roughly two weeks working time to produce the score, against continuing uncertainties about whether the premiere would actually go ahead or whether the censors might change their minds again.[73] To this end General von Seeckt wrote immediately to the Minister of the Interior in a letter marked 'Secret':

I see the authorization of this film, now as before, as imposing an extremely serious and unnecessary strain on military discipline and public peace and order. I am certain of your agreement and support when I therefore appeal to you to use every possible means – for instance, referring the case to the Reich Chief Prosecutor for him to deal with – to prevent the performance.[74]

Three days later, on 15 April, he issued a military order banning German soldiers from going to see the film on the grounds that it could undermine discipline.[75] This echoed the old pre-1914 imperial order banning soldiers from becoming members of the Social Democratic Party: old habits do indeed die hard.

Behind the scenes further attempts were made to prevent the premiere. The owners of the major Berlin cinemas, reacting partly to commercial pressure from the largest German cinema concern, Ufa, partly to political pressure and a reluctance to show a 'tendentious film', and partly to a genuine fear of disturbances, refused at first to make their cinemas available to show the film.[76] The Reich Cabinet, conscious of the fact that the censorship office had approved the showing of *Potemkin* by a majority of only one vote against the strongly felt opposition of both the War Ministry and the Ministry of the Interior, met in secret session on 28 April and asked the Supreme State Prosecutor whether those responsible for the exhibition and distribution of *Potemkin* might be arraigned for high treason.[77] His advice was that banning the film might cause more disturbances than screening it, but this view was communicated to the Prussian Prime Minister Otto Braun and the Berlin Chief of Police only on the morning of the premiere, 29 April 1926.[78] In the company of the Supreme State Prosecutor, the Prussian Minister of Culture and 'several gentlemen from the Reich Chancellery with a suitable retinue' both men immediately visited the Apollo theatre, a former music hall on Friedrichstraße, where the premiere was to be held.[79] The organizers made a favourable impression on their distinguished visitors and the screening went ahead.

Three days earlier, on 26 April, Eisenstein and Tisse had finally run out of money: their living 'like aristocrats' had come to an end and they had returned to Moscow by train. When they got home Eisenstein found a telegram waiting for him from the Soviet ambassador in Berlin. He asked the director to return to Berlin for the premiere of his film: the only way that Eisenstein could have reached Berlin in time was by air, but the flight was cancelled because of bad weather, so that he had to rely on eye-witness reports.[80]

The Battleship Potemkin was received enthusiastically on the left and centre-left, and the critics were almost unanimous in their view that a turning point in the history of cinema had been reached. Prometheus wrote to Eisenstein on 1 June, after he had complained about their lack of communication:

The press showing was a really tremendous experience. As you know we had commissioned a special score from the composer

23. Advertisement for *Potemkin* in Münzenberg's German illustrated weekly

Edmund Meisel. It was this score that helped the film to its greatest triumph. In parts the music was so powerful that, combined with the images on the screen, it had such an effect on the audience that their inner excitement made them hold on tightly to their seats. The music is particularly impressive in the Steps sequence and again when the 'Potemkin' is preparing for battle. People felt as if they were literally on board the ship, so convincing was the imitation of the beat and rhythm of the machines. What you yourself envisaged as the music for *Potemkin* has been fully realized.[81]

Prometheus sent a copy of the score to Moscow but their suggestion for a Moscow performance was never realized in Eisenstein's lifetime and a visit by Meisel to conduct it in November 1927 made no difference.[82] The critical reaction in Berlin to the score at least was however unambiguous. The director Carl Junghans later recalled:

It may be that Eisenstein gave Meisel a few instructions, but the synchronization with the film is Meisel. Things like the silence before the engines start may possibly be traced back to Eisenstein, because he himself was a very musical man. On the other hand Meisel was also a technically incredibly experienced bandleader for whom synchronizing from the rostrum presented no difficulties whatsoever. With his twenty-five musicians he accompanied up to six performances a day, playing from eleven in the morning until late at night. I think that 35 per cent of the [film's] success, if not more, was on account of the music.[83]

Even the German Foreign Minister, Gustav Stresemann, later suggested that the film might not have been so dangerous had it been shown without Meisel's score.[84]

Potemkin however was not yet home and dry even in Germany. On the one hand sympathetic critics enthused about the film. Not surprisingly the cheerleader in the campaign of support was the German Communist Party newspaper *Die rote Fahne*, whose critic Otto Steinicke enthused, rather appropriately, on May Day:

The suspense amongst the audience is discharged in a roar of thunderous applause. (Even for the spectator who is not a member of the proletariat. Even he is completely guzzled down and swallowed up by the superbly structured treatment, by the most marvellous magnificent film that we have ever seen.) Your innermost feelings are stirred. Every nerve vibrates. What an experience that was!

24. The opening bars of Meisel's music for *Potemkin*

This film could only have come from Soviet Russia, with the victory of the proletariat, the hegemony of a class that has everything to gain, not just in one country but in the whole world! *The Battleship Potemkin* is the first masterpiece in a film series that will depict before our very eyes and bring to life the struggles of 1905.

Even though this work of art, which has no 'stars' in it, appears to have been mutilated by the censors (through its censorship our 'democracy' has trimmed the red flag from the 'Potemkin's' mast, faded out individual scenes and glossed over the wall of Cossacks trampling everyone on the steps by the harbour in Odessa, treading on a child, and so on), this has left no gaping hole: we see everything, we feel everything that has been excised ... and form it all into a single whole![85]

Other, less politically committed critics, echoed Steinicke's enthusiasm. In *Die literarische Welt* Willy Haas praised the film for its aesthetic, rather than its purely political virtues:

Nothing, nothing at all happens in this film. Suddenly every heart is burning. ... I cannot imagine anyone leaving this film without being shaken by it, a film in which nobody plays a 'role', because there is no role and no plot in it at all. Here we really do have 'film rhetoric' liberated ... a rhetoric that does not argue, that does not have to prove anything, and that does not speak at all ... except through the sound of the bare image-word, which overwhelms film language.[86]

Alfred Polgar took a similar line:

Many people see in the 'spirit of collectivism' that gave birth to the film the particular secret of its effect. But it seems to me that this secret lies in the artistic rather than the political sphere, in the fact that the man who made *Potemkin* has not translated narrative into images, but has thought, felt and conceived in images. *Here film is speaking its mother tongue.*[87]

F. W. Murnau, whose *Faust* set Eisenstein had visited, was reported as having confessed that 'he had not liked the beginning very much but, as the plot developed, he was so gripped and infected by the general mood that he was prepared to grab his revolver, throw himself into the sailors' struggle and shoot.'[88] Fritz Lang was reported to have had to reconsider his approach to *Metropolis* as a result of seeing *Potemkin*.[89] Last but not least the eminent stage director Max Reinhardt is said to have remarked, 'Now for the first time I am ready to admit that theatre will have to give way to film.'[90]

Critics on the political right, on the other hand, were deeply, sometimes virulently hostile. In the nationalist press the audience was characterized as 'the nocturnal dregs of Berlin', while the film itself was described as 'the bloodthirsty film' and 'the blood film'.[91] The nationalist Stahlhelm veterans' organization placed a newspaper advertisement warning its members against 'seeing this Soviet-Jewish propaganda film ... Don't pay out money for this sort of subversive and unpatriotic rubbish!'[92] The censorship office and the political and legal authorities also came under attack for their apparent complacency, as in this report in the *Berliner Lokal-Anzeiger* under the heading 'The Murder Film from Moscow':

> Then comes the height of brutality, the Odessa bloodbath and we are spared not a single drop of red blood. The timpanist in the orchestra pit assails our eardrums while on the screen we see men, women and children collapsing under a hail of bullets from the Cossacks. The stench of blood spread through the auditorium, making men into beasts. Women scream, the citizen who has to see everything turns pale and the man with the red tie utters cries of rage. But the Chief of Police, who could take note of these effects, looks calmly on, as a wind is sown that will reap the whirlwind.[93]

Early attempts were made to close the cinema because of overcrowding, but this danger was overcome by numbering the tickets and designating them for a particular performance. Nonetheless the Berlin police kept a close eye on the proceedings.[94] *Agents-provocateurs* attempted to disrupt performances so that a renewed ban could be justified on public order grounds, while a group calling themselves the 'German Sailors' Club' threatened to attack the cinema with hand grenades if the film were not taken off.[95] Nevertheless the film proved more and more popular and performances were increasingly sold out completely in advance. The War Ministry reported that in one suburb 'five obviously German men' dressed as sailors were parading outside the cinema to advertise the film, wearing the old German naval uniform with 'Potemkin' written on their headbands, a clear sign of subversion and a threat to public order!'[96] Prometheus informed Eisenstein that this kind of approach was part of their fight back against the right-wing offensive. Presumably fearing a reimposition of the ban, they had tried to distribute the film as quickly and widely as possible. Almost immediately after its premiere the distributors had been 'besieged by a veritable storm of cinema owners' so that *Potemkin* was showing at 25 cinemas in Berlin and within a fortnight a total of 45 copies had been made available for exhibition. By the beginning of June 1926 the film was showing in 'almost all Germany's large cities'.[97]

This tactic can only have enraged the right-wing opposition further. Shortly after the premiere the German Cabinet met again to discuss the film. They resolved that 'all possible measures must be taken to prevent the wider exhibition of this film'. The Foreign Minister and former Chancellor, Gustav Stresemann, wrote to the Prussian Prime Minister, Otto Braun, urging him to take action:

I am getting reports from all sides that frenetic applause breaks out whenever there is some action directed against the officers, who are portrayed as brutal, and that in working-class areas people who do not want to applaud are beaten up until they stand up and join in the demonstration. Film is the most effective propaganda medium in existence today. It can be far more effective than meetings or theatrical performances because it reaches hundreds of thousands and millions.[98]

Prime Minister Braun seems to have thought Stresemann's concerns to be the product of 'exaggerated anxiety' but others were less sanguine. On 12 June the conservative provincial government of Württemberg applied to the supreme film censor's office in Berlin for a reimposition of the ban on the grounds that the film presented an evident and continuing threat to law and order. Support also came from the governments of Bavaria, Hesse and Thuringia.[99] The Left organized a counterattack and recruited Albert Einstein (who had reputedly been 'stunned' by the film), Erwin Piscator, Alfred Kerr and a host of others to their cause. Intellectuals rallied at a protest meeting held in the Hotel Piccadilly in late June at which the last speaker argued:

Potemkin's success without newspaper advertisements and the propaganda of the star system signifies a change in public taste. It has tired of American potboilers, of 'blonde Rhine maidens' and patriotic films with their falsifications of history in which war is constantly presented as spectacle.

Potemkin was the first truth. Now we have to organize the public.[100]

As part of that effort the meeting closed with a screening of the film, with Edmund Meisel conducting the orchestra performing his dynamic score!

The protests were initially in vain and on 12 July the film was banned for a second time. Following another round of protests the decision was rescinded on 27 July, but this time the censors insisted on a further 100 metres of cuts, so that the emasculated film could be seen by adults and juveniles alike. One left-wing critic saw this as a pyrrhic victory:

> You can argue about changes in the text, but not about cuts in the visuals. It is true that at the beginning you can still see a sleeping sailor tossing and turning in torment. Why? Perhaps he is dreaming about something unpleasant and you wait for the familiar picture that should appear at this point – 'My home is my happiness' with the sailor at home by the cradle of his new-born child – because the stroke of the lash that rained down on him has been cut out. Neither the officers nor even the ship's doctor are thrown into the water, and the pince-nez no longer dangle from a rope. And the Cossacks? They still march down the steps. But do they open fire? That you no longer see. Do they kill anybody? All that happened in days gone by. Now the crowd disperses harmlessly. The director is Buchowetzki.[101] Almost all the close-ups have gone.
>
> The entire structure, the phenomenal upsurge in the action, the cross-cutting between close-up and mass shots, the contrast between the menacingly calm march of the Cossacks and the alarmed population, the rhythm, the inflammatory power – all this has been lost. The best proof of the merits of the film and the mediocrity of its re-editing lies in the fact that the destruction of its humane ideology has also meant the loss of its artistic qualities. For Germany, Eisenstein's work is dead. It is precisely because the effect of the film has been so precisely calculated and composed that you can make cuts only with great care (as happened with the first German version). The newly re-edited version is even worse than the frequently ridiculous editions of the classics produced for high schools and girls' boarding schools. For those who fought for this film, there is nothing more that can be done with this cripple.[102]

But, even in this 'crippled' state *Potemkin* was still a thorn in the flesh of the political right. A renewed appeal to the censors led to a final decision to uphold its release in censored form but to restrict the audience in future to adults.[103] Prometheus produced a sound version using Meisel's score in 1930 that was another 100 metres shorter. Between the version shown at the Bolshoi Theatre in December 1925 (1,740 m.) and that still in circulation when the Nazis came to power (1,353 m.) the crippled German version of *Potemkin* had lost almost a quarter of its footage.

Despite its travails with the censors, or perhaps at least in part because of them, Eisenstein's film had an enormous impact on those Germans who saw it. Bertolt Brecht made it in the focus of a poem, Lion Feuchtwanger devoted a chapter of his novel *Success* to it and German film-makers even produced a number of their own 'battleship' films.[104] If much of the debate and manoeuvring in 1926 had been *politically* inspired, it is nonetheless true that *The Battleship Potemkin* became an *aesthetic* reference point for the cultural life of the Berlin left-wing intelligentsia in that decade. The leading critic and cultural theorist, Walter Benjamin, later observed:

> *Potemkin* is a great film and a rare achievement. It is a sign of despair to protest about precisely this fact. There is enough bad tendentious art around, including bad tendentious art that is socialist. Those works are defined by their effect, count on worn reflexes and make use of clichés. This film, however, is set in ideological concrete, accurately calculated in every detail like the arch of a bridge. The more powerfully the blows hammer down on it, the better the arch resounds. Whoever shakes it with kid gloves will hear and move nothing.[105]

Nonetheless Erwin Piscator, whose later stage productions were profoundly influenced by the film, was later highly critical of Eisenstein's basic method. Writing in January 1928, he argued:

> In an article recently disseminated through the German press the *Potemkin* director S. M. Eisenstein declared, *inter alia*, that he saw the task of the *Potemkin* film as to electrify and rouse the masses. If that were really the only task of revolutionary drama, this effect could just as well be achieved by staging a boxing match, a race or any kind of military parade. Proletarian political theatre might as well give up if it wanted to appeal only to primitive instincts and emotions. This theatre in particular can only have an effect if it is

able to convince, to release and mobilize the spiritual energies of the masses.

It will not achieve this aim through the psychology of Freud or Pavlov, as Eisenstein argues, but through the application of Marxist philosophy. We do not want just to enthuse: we want to communicate clarity and insight. We therefore always begin at the beginning and, by elaborating historical truth and revealing every problem in its complete context and rigorously pursuing this, we demonstrate to the masses the inevitability of the fate we are depicting and the only way to overcome it. For me the principal weakness in *Potemkin* lies in the fact that Eisenstein is satisfied with depicting the mutiny on a ship, instead of situating this episode in the context of all the revolutionary forces of 1905. Theatre is far superior to film as a vehicle for the revelation of the complete context. It is precisely the link between film and stage, between epic black-and-white art and the drama of the spoken word and three-dimensional people, that seems to me to provide the most important means of achieving this goal.[106]

But it was not only those on the left who were impressed: so too was Joseph Goebbels, who was to become Nazi Gauleiter of Berlin in November 1926 and Hitler's one and only propaganda minister in February 1933. In his first ministerial speech to German film-makers two weeks after taking office, he called on them to produce a German equivalent. Much to Eisenstein's chagrin, Goebbels argued:

It is a fantastically well-made film and displays considerable cinematic artistry. The decisive factor is its orientation. Someone with no firm ideological convictions could be turned into a Bolshevik by this film. This proves that a political outlook can be very well contained in a work of art and that even the worst outlook can be conveyed if this is done through the medium of an outstanding work of art.[107]

For better or worse, the explosive combination of *Potemkin* and Berlin in the 1920s had put both Eisenstein and Soviet film on the world cultural map.

After the enthusiastic reception in Moscow and the tumultuous one in Berlin, the reaction in London was very much that of the traditional stiff upper lip. In the UK films were conventionally submitted to the

British Board of Film Censors, a non-statutory body established by the industry itself in 1913. Its judgements had no legal force, but were usually accepted at the national level, although, because of a quirk in the law, they could be overturned at the local level by the watch committees, which were responsible for fire and public safety.[108] The Board had grown in status since its establishment and attributed this, at least in part, to its unspoken policy of avoiding anything that was politically controversial. In October 1925 the BBFC had insisted on cutting 1,250 metres from an anti-Soviet film, *Red Russia*, which had caused disturbances in both France and the Netherlands.[109] In May 1926 a strike by coal miners had developed into the UK's first (and so far last) General Strike, reviving fears in the Conservative government of the time of a revolution like that in Russia and of infiltration through the efforts of the Communist International. The Establishment was fortified in its resolve by a report in *The Times* of the difficulties that Eisenstein's film had caused in Germany:

The action of the Berlin police in permitting this film to be represented has given rise to much discussion. It is a filmed reproduction of the mutiny on the Russian cruiser of that name which took place in 1905. It is travestied by sentimentality and prejudice and is full of bloodthirsty scenes on board the cruiser and shooting and panic in Odessa. Though its naval technique is full of palpable absurdities, it has an extraordinary effect on the public, which takes sides in the theatre, as the film shows infuriated sailors murdering their officers. Its propaganda effects may be doubted. Perhaps some part of the opposition to it is prompted by painful memories of the treatment of German officers at the time of the Revolution, and some part of the intemperate applause by equally painful memories on the other side.[110]

It was against this background that *The Battleship Potemkin* was submitted to the BBFC.

The censor chosen to view the film was Col. J. C. Hanna DSO, who had joined the BBFC four years earlier after a distinguished military career including colonial service in India and Ireland. As his background might suggest, Hanna was not at all sympathetic to subversive films of any kind and he consulted the Home Secretary, Sir William Joynson-Hicks, who was even less sympathetic and, like all too many members of the British Establishment at that time – and indeed since – hostile to cinema as a serious medium, let alone as an art form. Not surprisingly, on 30 September 1926, *The Battleship Potemkin* was banned for public exhibition in the United Kingdom.[111] But that was by no means the end of the story, given the peculiar legal situation.

In 1928 Herbert Wilcox was able successfully to defy both the BBFC and the Foreign Office over *Dawn*, his film about the trial and execution of Edith Cavell for espionage in 1915.[112] In his campaign, the Irish-born Wilcox had received vociferous support from his fellow Irishman George Bernard Shaw, who also vehemently objected to the continuing ban on *Potemkin*:

It has nothing to do with the morals of the film; it is simply a move in class warfare. The screen may wallow in every extremity of vulgarity and villainy provided it whitewashes authority. But let it shew a single fleck on the whitewash, and no excellence, moral, pictorial, or histrionic, can save it from prompt suppression and defamation. That is what censorship means.[113]

Following Wilcox's success Ivor Montagu, a Communist activist and film producer, submitted *Potemkin* to the two local authorities responsible for the capital, the London and Middlesex County Councils. Both councils, controlled by the Conservatives, upheld the BBFC ban on the grounds of the film's alleged violence. In a leaflet published shortly afterwards, Montagu claimed that he had intended to submit the film to other local authorities but that, following a visit from officers from Scotland Yard, the distributors had declined to supply copies even for private (or club) performance without the express permission of the Home Secretary, which was not forthcoming. Public exhibition was now clearly impossible, but a closed club performance, not subject to the same censorship procedures, remained a possibility if a copy of the film could be obtained from another source. Montagu persevered and eventually received a print from the Soviet trade delegation in Berlin, which was shown to a London Film Society audience at the Tivoli Palace in London's Strand on Sunday, 10 November 1929. Edmund Meisel conducted his own score at the performance: it does not appear to have made the same impression in London as it had done in Berlin, but then Britain was still regarded at that time as '*das Land ohne Musik*' (the land without music).[114]

The review that appeared in *The Times* two days later almost beggars belief as a classic example both of muddled thinking and of a critic missing the point, but it characterizes so effectively the prevailing attitude towards film that I reproduce it here in full:

The Battleship Potemkin disappoints most of the hopes which the censor's ban has aroused. As a historical record it is too distorted to have any value, even though the distortion is frequently in the direction of truth: as propaganda it is vastly inferior to The End of St Petersburg; and as a film it is no better than the average Soviet film.

But in film matters the Soviet average is a high one, and Potemkin, although one of the earliest, illustrates many of the methods which distinguish Soviet films from those of any other country. Some of these, for instance such symbolic captions as 'Men and Worms' are as childish as those of the early American films. But they are counteracted by an admirable restraint, which, unlike that of German producers, does not lead to lifelessness. The mutiny on board the battleship offered opportunities for alarums and excursions which no Western producer would have been able to resist. In this film only one shot is fired.

The necessary effect of action and excitement is given by the alternating rhythm which all Soviet film producers seek, but few achieve. First the confused mass: then one of the individuals in the mass, expressing alone the feelings which the producer wishes to convey. Then, before the individual becomes too prominent, a reversion to the mass. The method is seen at its best in the scenes where revolutionary orators harangue the mob on the quayside. First we are shown an orator working himself into a fury; then two or three individuals from the mob in close-up. It is the reverse of the American method, where everything is expressed through the individual. It is also a significant commentary on life in Soviet Russia, where, according to more than one observer, the individual has long been swallowed in the mass.

The scenes which cause public exhibition of Potemkin to be prohibited are among the least satisfactory. In particular, the massacre of the citizens of Odessa, effective enough in itself, loses all reality from the omission of any mention of the riots and arson which were its immediate cause. The soldiers marching slowly down the flight of steps and firing at intervals on the crowd fleeing before them, give an impression of ruthless brutality which is all the greater from its restraint. But the derelict perambulator – hailed by Soviet critics as the supreme example of film symbolism – is an irrelevant appeal to irrelevant emotions. And when it is followed by the caption: 'To the brutality of the military authority the guns of the rebel battleship replied,' it becomes almost ridiculous.[115]

The adjacent column in *The Times* gave a clear indication of the cultural diet that the critic would presumably have found less ridiculous and Shaw would have found represented 'every extremity of vulgarity'. It included Gilbert and Sullivan's *Patience* at the Savoy; a new farce by Ben Travers; the Ivor Novello revue *The House that Jack Built*, starring Cicely Courtneidge and Jack Hulbert; the last week of a musical adaptation of Mark Twain's *A Yankee at the Court of King Arthur*, and Sean O'Casey's *The Silver Tassie*, which in that unchallenging company stuck out like another sore thumb. There were subsequently a small number of club screenings of *Potemkin* in Britain, including four in Hampstead in January 1934 alone, but Eisenstein's film remained banned for public exhibition until granted an X (for adults only) certificate by the BBFC in 1954.[116] By that time the decision was politically safe, partly because the commercial release of an almost 30-year-old silent film was unlikely to be a viable proposition, and partly because by then its message had been largely emasculated by the passage of time. In short it took until 1954 for the British censors to reach the stage of permissiveness that their German equivalents had reached in the summer of 1926.

In comparison with the excitement generated in Moscow, Berlin and, in a different way, London, the reception of *The Battleship Potemkin* elsewhere raised few surprises. The film was banned for public exhibition in France, as in Britain, until the 1950s but was more widely seen at private screenings because cinema was taken more seriously in France as an art form and as a cultural and political force, and the country consequently had a more highly developed film society movement under the auspices of the Ciné-Club de France. The premiere took place in Paris on 18 November 1926 without any musical accompaniment whatsoever.[117] The film director Marcel L'Herbier suggested that Eisenstein deserved a Nobel Prize, while the writer Colette expressed her 'highest exultation'.[118] The historian Georges Sadoul claimed that:

> The projection in film clubs of banned works by Pudovkin, Eisenstein and, above all, Dziga Vertov, played a determining role. *The Mother* or *Potemkin* demonstrated to the younger generation that

there was more poetry in a human face filmed in the street than in the mechanics or the geometric forms of abstract films, more art in montage than in the laborious search for poetic props.[119]

The critic Léon Moussinac remarked, 'At that stage in the life of cinema, the French première of *Potemkin* was a thunderbolt which takes on, in retrospect, exceptional historical importance.' He later recalled the event:

> As the images of violence succeeded one another in absolute silence, the atmosphere in the theatre became pregnant with tension. Even those who had come to protest felt themselves overcome by the truth of an action transfigured by Eisenstein's genius. In the end excitement was mixed with a kind of stupor. No one had ever seen a work so moving and expressive in its unity. The epiphany was complete.[120]

On 5 December 1926, after a three-week long scrutiny by the censors, *The Armored Cruiser Potemkin* (as it was released in the US) was first shown publicly at the Biltmore Theater in New York. It was proclaimed as an 'event' and 'the best film of the year', while Charlie Chaplin joined the earlier praise from his fellow United Artists, calling it quite simply 'the best film in the world'.[121] Following a preview screening *Photoplay Magazine* reported:

> There is no story to this film, or no leading actors. If you weren't told that it was staged, you'd swear it was a prehistoric newsreel. The photography is beautiful enough to enchant an artist and the action is vivid and swift enough to satisfy any box office demand for drama. The scene in which the Cossacks pursue the populace down a long flight of steps, shooting into the crowd, is unforgettably impressive. When enough of our directors have seen this episode, you'll find it duplicated in home-made dramas. And yet, alas, the ugly head of propaganda intrudes itself to mar an artistic triumph.[122]

The Hollywood producer David O. Selznick described *Potemkin* as 'unquestionably one of the greatest motion pictures ever made' and 'gripping beyond words – its vivid and realistic reproduction of a bit of history being far more interesting than could any film of fiction; and this simply because of the genius of its production and direction.' He

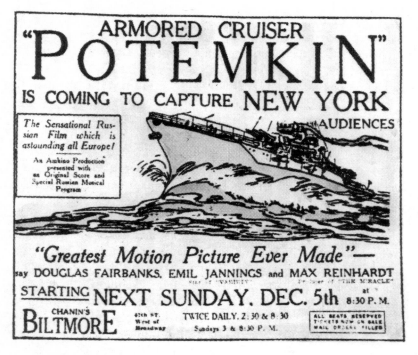

25. Advertising *Potemkin* in the USA

urged MGM to procure the services of 'the man responsible for it, a young director named Eisenstein'.[123] The *New Yorker* endorsed *Potemkin* too: 'So truly is it acted and so intelligently is it directed that it becomes an event lifted from history and placed before your eyes, and marks another step in the march of the motion picture toward a serious place among the arts. Do not fail to go and see it.'[124]

The Battleship Potemkin secured for itself and for its young director a unique place in the history of cinema. Neither could subsequently be ignored by anyone who took the medium seriously and, broadly speaking, neither has been by anyone who has done. The British documentary film-maker Paul Rotha, writing *The Film Till Now* in 1930, recognized that '*Potemkin* marked a new era in the technique of the cinema',[125] while his associate John Grierson regarded Eisenstein as 'the greatest master of public spectacle in the history of the cinema'.[126] Grierson also cited a rather bizarre and amusing observation by Rudyard Kipling when he saw the film: 'These Russians are doing all over again what we do so splendidly in our own country.

They are making tattoos, and what we ought to be doing ourselves is making tattoos in film form.'[127]

In a series of international surveys of film directors and critics *Potemkin* has persistently emerged as one of the most highly regarded films in cinema history. The first of these surveys was conducted by the Belgian Cinémathèque in 1952 to determine the ten best films of all time. Sixty-three *directors* selected *Potemkin* and the individual directors who chose it as their own personal favourite included both Elia Kazan and Billy Wilder while for Robert Bresson, Carl Dreyer and Luchino Visconti Eisenstein's film came third, for Luís Buñuel fourth, Orson Welles sixth and Vittorio De Sica eighth.[128] In 1958 at the film festival accompanying the Brussels World Fair, at which the previously suppressed Part 2 of Eisenstein's *Ivan the Terrible* [Ivan Groznyi, USSR, 1943–8] was finally given its Western premiere, a jury of 117 film *historians* from 26 countries selected 12 films which were then shown as the 'Best Films of All Time'. *Potemkin* came first – as the best film of all time – with 100 votes, followed by both Chaplin's *The Gold Rush* [USA, 1925] and De Sica's *Bicycle Thieves* [Ladri di biciclette, Italy, 1948] with 85 votes each. As best director Chaplin beat Eisenstein into second place with 250 votes to 168, with René Clair in third place at 135. A second jury of young *film-makers* decided, after ten hours of debate, that the 12 films 'should not be measured against each other' and eventually selected six films as having 'a living and lasting value'. These six included *Potemkin*.[129]

Since 1952 the British Film Institute's journal *Sight and Sound* has conducted a similar survey amongst film *critics* every ten years. In 1952 *Potemkin* came fourth (*Bicycle Thieves* came first). In 1962 it came sixth, alongside *Bicycle Thieves* and Eisenstein's *Ivan the Terrible*, with Orson Welles's *Citizen Kane* [USA, 1941] first, while Eisenstein was voted best director with 46 votes, beating Chaplin by three votes and Jean Renoir by 11.[130] In 1972, however, *Potemkin* had risen to third place, behind *Citizen Kane* and Renoir's *La Règle du jeu* [France, 1939], even though Eisenstein had slipped to fifth, ceding first place to Welles.[131] In 1982 the film had slipped back to sixth place again, with *Citizen Kane* and *La Règle du jeu* occupying the first two places, and Eisenstein had disappeared from the list of directors altogether, leaving Welles, Renoir and – perhaps surprisingly – Chaplin in the first three places.[132] In 1992 *Sight and Sound* decided to test the views of both critics and directors. In the critics' top ten films *Potemkin* still came sixth, with *Citizen Kane* and *La Règle du jeu* still at the head of the list, while Eisenstein reappeared at the bottom of the list of directors, with Welles and Renoir again coming out on top, and Jean-Luc Godard and Alfred Hitchcock overtaking Chaplin! But in 1992 both the film and its director were absent from the two lists drawn up by film directors, a fate also shared by Renoir and his film.[133] Nevertheless, despite its changing fortunes in the critics' taste, *The Battleship Potemkin* is the *only* film to have appeared in *all* these five lists spanning 40 years of cinema history.

Such lists are, of course, problematic, since it is never entirely certain precisely what they measure or how precisely they measure it. At best the notion of the 'ten best' represents a trivial pursuit, but at worst it not merely measures, but also confirms and fixes the prevailing view of the established canon. In response to the question, 'Does the cinema canon really matter?' Ian Christie has persuasively argued:

> To those who think this is just a harmless game, I would say, 'think again'. Not only does the canon directly govern what future genera-tions of students will learn about, but indirectly it affects what is bought for television, what's programmed in cinematheques and repertory cinemas, what's released on video, what appears in cinema-related publishing and, perhaps most important, what archives prioritize and preserve. Anyone who doubts that the cinema canon is a powerful reality has about as much imagination as the Lumière brothers, who doubted their invention had a future.[134]

For a broader public, however, which thinks that *Star Wars* [USA, 1977, dir. George Lucas] and *Titanic* [USA, 1998, dir. James Cameron] are the two greatest films ever made,[135] *Potemkin* as a film remains at best a name to conjure with, at worst a completely unknown quantity. If this small book has done something to retrieve this historic and influ-ential film from its undeserved public obscurity, it will have more than achieved its purpose.

Notes

1 The Art, at the city-centre end of the Arbat, is still in use as a first-run cinema today. It is situated just across Vozdvizhenka Street from the former mansion where Eisenstein and Alexandrov had worked with the Proletkult on *Wise Man* in 1923.
2 K & L, p. 210.
3 e.g. *Pravda*, 4 February and 17 January 1926 respectively.
4 *Kinogazeta*, 16 February 1926, cited in: K & L, p. 215, Marshall, p. 101.

5 Advertisement reproduced in: K & L, p. 187.

6 R. Taylor, *The Politics of the Soviet Cinema 1917–1929*, Cambridge, 1979, pp. 95–6.

7 Edmund Meisel conducted a private performance of his accompanying score for them: Bulgakowa, p. 86.

8 *Die rote Fahne*, 7 May 1926, cited in: K & L, pp. 231–2.

9 e.g. A. Lagorno, 'Meri Pikford i Duglas Ferbenks o *Potemkine*' [Mary Pickford and Douglas Fairbanks on *Potemkin*], *Sovetskii ekran*, 8 June 1926. What the radical Lef group called the 'Pickfordization' of Soviet cinema was the subject of at least three Soviet films of the period: a two-reel parody of Fairbanks in *The Thief of Bagdad* made for the Kultkino studio in 1925: *The Thief, but not of Bagdad* [Vor, a ne bagdadskii], Sergei Komarov's *The Kiss from Mary Pickford* [Potselui Meri Pikford, 1927] and Nikolai Khodataev's animated short *One of Many* [Odna iz mnogikh, 1927]. While *Potemkin* was being made, Khodataev had also completed an anniversary film, another animated short, *1905–1925*.

10 Cited in: V. B. Shklovskii, *Eizenshtein*, Moscow, 1973, p. 133.

11 Khrisanf Khersonskii, 'Kinointerventsiia' [A Cinematic Intervention], *Pravda*, 2 June 1926.

12 Bulgakowa, p. 81.

13 K & L, p. 219.

14 *Vechernie izvestiia*, 9 September 1926, cited in: K & L, p. 219.

15 D. G., 'Oshibka Goskino', *Krasnaia gazeta*, 28 October 1926; K & L, p. 220. The translation here is my own: cf. Marshall, pp. 105–6.

16 *Trud*, 1 January 1926, cited in: K & L, p. 196; cf Marshall, pp. 94–5.

17 *Sovetskii ekran*, 1926, no. 1, cited in: K & L, pp. 211–12; cf Marshall, pp. 247–9.

18 PRIM., 'Svoe litso' [Our Own Face], *Vecherniaia Moskva*, 12 January 1926, cited in: K & L, pp. 212–13; cf. Marshall, pp. 245–6.

19 Viacheslav K. Viskovsky (1881–1933) was known for making melodramas on revolutionary themes: *Under the Debris of Empire* [Pod oblomkami imperii] and *Let Us Renounce the Old World* [Otrechemsia ot starogo mira, both 1917] and what Eisenstein was later to denounce as 'drawing-room dramas' such as *Little Cady* [Malen'kaia Kadi, 1918]. In 1920 he went to work in Hollywood but returned to the USSR to make *Red Partisans* [Krasnye partizany, 1924], *The Ninth of January* and *Minaret of Death* [Minaret smerti, both 1925]. The cameraman for *The Ninth of January* was Andrei Moskvin, who was to work for most of his career with the FEKS group in Leningrad but who later acted as director of interior photography on Eisenstein's *Ivan the Terrible* [Ivan Groznyi, 1943–8]. The script was written by Petr Shchegolev from the Leningrad Party History Institute, but in 1925 this did not yet guarantee it a favourable reception.

20 *Kinogazeta*, 12 January 1926, cited in: K & L, p. 213.

21 Adrian I. Piotrovsky (1898–1938) was purged a year after being dismissed from his Leningrad post. He is one of those shadowy administrative figures in Soviet cinema whose background influence was

pp. 3–18; D. Hartshough, 'Soviet Film Distribution and Exhibition in Germany, 1921–1933', *Historical Journal of Film, Radio & Television*, vol. 5, no. 2 (1985), pp. 131–48. For an account of Münzenberg's activities, see: S. Koch, *Double Lives. Stalin, Willi Münzenberg and the Seduction of the Intellectuals*, London, 1996.

62 E. Eyck, *A History of the Weimar Republic*, Cambridge MA and London, 1962, vol. 1, p. 150.

63 H. Herlinghaus [G. Kherlingkhauz], '*Bronenosets Potemkin* pered sudom germanskoi burzhuaznoi tsenzury' [*The Battleship Potemkin* on Trial by German Bourgeois Censorship], *Iz istorii kino 3*, Moscow, 1960, pp. 104–5.

64 E. Piscator, *The Political Theatre*, London, 1980, p. 357.

65 Eyck, vol. 2, pp. 92–3.

66 G. Kühn, K. Tümmler and W. Wimmer (eds), *Film und revolutionäre Arbeiterbewegung in Deutschland 1918–1945* [Film and the Revolutionary Workers' Movement in Germany 1918–45], Berlin GDR, 1975, vol. 1, pp. 323–4; K & L, pp. 223–4.

67 The letter of authorization from Mikhail Kapchinsky, director of the Goskino studio, dated 22 February, is reproduced in: O. Bulgakowa (ed.), *Eisenstein und Deutschland*, Berlin, 1998, p. 71.

68 Bulgakowa, *Eisenstein und Deutschland*, pp. 71–2.

69 Edmund Meisel (1894–1930) later composed several other film scores, most notably for Arnold Fanck's mountain picture *The Holy Mountain* [Der heilige Berg, Germany 1926, starring Leni Riefenstahl], Walter Ruttmann's famous documentary *Berlin. Symphony of a City* [Berlin. Die Sinfonie der Großstadt, Germany 1927] and the German release version of Eisenstein's *October* [Oktiabr', 1927]. In 1928 he worked in London on a synchronized score for the English-language version of Friedrich Zelnick's *The Crimson Circle*, an Edgar Wallace adaptation. See: W. Sudendorf, *Der Stummfilmmusiker Edmund Meisel* [The Silent Film Musician Edmund Meisel], Frankfurt am Main, 1984.

70 The translation is my own but cf.: S. M. Eisenstein, 'Organic Unity and Pathos', in: *Nonindifferent Nature* (ed. H. Marshall), Cambridge, 1987, pp. 32–3.

71 *ESW1*, pp. 113–14; *ER*, pp. 80–1; *FF*, pp. 234–5.

72 Kühn, p. 330; K & L, pp. 226–7; Marshall, pp. 119–21.

73 Sudendorf, *Edmund Meisel*, p. 14.

74 Kühn, p. 332.

75 Kühn, p. 332.

76 Telegram from Prometheus to Eisenstein, 16 April 1926, cited in: Bulgakowa, *Eisenstein und Deutschland*, pp. 74–5.

77 G. Stresemann, *Vermächtnis. Der Nachlass in drei Bänden* [The Legacy. Unpublished Works in 3 Volumes], Berlin, 1932, vol. 2, p. 408.

78 Herlinghaus, p. 106.

79 Letter from Prometheus to Eisenstein, 1 June 1926, cited in: Bulgakowa, *Eisenstein und Deutschland*, p. 76.

80 Bulgakowa, *Eisenstein*, p. 84.

81 Bulgakowa, *Eisenstein und Deutschland*, pp. 76–7.

82 Sudendorf, *Edmund Meisel*, p. 75.
83 Cited in: Sudendorf, *Edmund Meisel*, p. 15.
84 Stresemann, vol. 2, p. 408.
85 O. Steinicke, '*Panzerkreuzer Potemkin*', *Die rote Fahne*, 1 May 1926, cited in: Kühn, p. 336.
86 W. Haas, 'Meine Meinung' [My Opinion], *Die literarische Welt*, 1926, no. 19, cited in: Sudendorf, *Eisenstein*, p. 67.
87 A. Polgar, '*Panzerkreuzer Potemkin*', *Das Tagebuch*, 1926, no. 22, cited in: Sudendorf, *Eisenstein*, p. 68.
88 Letter from Ufa employee Leo Witlin to Eisenstein, 3 May 1926, K & L, p. 230.
89 Letter from Witlin to Eisenstein, 5 May 1926, K & L, p. 230.
90 Cited in an advertising leaflet produced by Amkino for the US premiere in New York in 1926; K & L, p. 231.
91 *Deutsche Allgemeine Zeitung* and *Berliner Lokal-Anzeiger* coverage cited in: Sudendorf, *Eisenstein*, p. 69.
92 Loc. cit.
93 'Der Mordfilm aus Moskau', *Berliner Lokal-Anzeiger*, 8 May 1926, cited in: Sudendorf, *Eisenstein*, p. 69.
94 Kühn, pp. 337–42.
95 Sudendorf, *Eisenstein*, p. 69.
96 Kühn, p. 343.
97 Bulgakowa, *Eisenstein und Deutschland*, p. 77.
98 Stresemann, vol. 2, p. 408.
99 K & L, p. 238; Marshall, pp. 133–4.
100 'Protest gegen die Potemkin-Hetze' [Protest against the *Potemkin* Hate Campaign], *Der Montag Morgen*, 28 June 1926, cited in: K & L, p. 241; Marshall, p. 136.
101 Dimitri Buchowetzki (1885–1932) left Russia after the October Revolution and made a series of costume dramas with Emil Jannings and Pola Negri. His career foundered after a spell in Hollywood in the mid-1920s.
102 *Berliner Börsencourier*, 28 July 1926, cited in: K & L, p. 246, cf. Marshall, pp. 143–4.
103 Kühn, pp. 366–8.
104 Sudendorf, *Eisenstein*, p. 70. The Brecht and Feuchtwanger works are reproduced in: Marshall, pp. 355–62.
105 W. Benjamin, 'Erwiderung an Oscar A.H. Schmitz' [Reply to Oscar Schmitz], *Die literarische Welt*, 11 March 1927, reprinted in: R. Tiedemann & H. Schweppenhäuser (eds), *Walter Benjamin: Gesammelte Schriften* [Collected Writings], vol. II.2, p. 755.
106 E. Piscator, 'Bühne der Gegenwart und Zukunft' [The Present and Future Stage], *Die rote Fahne*, 1 January 1928, cited in: L. Hoffmann (ed.), *Erwin Piscator. Theater, Film, Politik*, Berlin GDR, 1980, pp. 48–9. Piscator later made a film himself, *The Revolt of the Fishermen* [Der Aufstand der Fischer; Vosstanie rybakov, USSR, 1934].
107 Cited in: R. Taylor, *Film Propaganda: Soviet Russia & Nazi Germany*, 2nd

edn, London & New York, 1998, p. 144. Eisenstein's angry response is translated in: *ESW1*, pp. 280–4.

108 There was, however, continuing pressure for the government to take central responsibility for film censorship. On 18 November 1926, in response to a backbencher's question, the then Home Secretary, Sir William Joynson-Hicks, argued that there was 'not sufficient evidence that the present system of censorship (which I would point out includes an important element of control by local authorities) fails to secure on the whole an adequate standard'; *Hansard*, vol. 199, col. 1979.

109 J. C. Robertson, *The Hidden Cinema. British Film Censorship in Action, 1913–1972*, London and New York, 1989, pp. 28–9.

110 'Plans of German Extremists. Communist Rally in Berlin. Police Leave Stopped', *The Times*, 21 May 1926, p. 16.

111 Robertson, p. 30; cf *Hansard*, vol. 214, cols 1209–10, 8 March 1928.

112 J. C. Robertson, '*Dawn* (1928): Edith Cavell and Anglo-German Relations', *Historical Journal of Film, Radio & Television*, vol. 4, no. 1 (March 1984), pp. 15–28.

113 G. B. Shaw, 'Views on the Censorship', *The British Film Journal*, April/May 1928, reproduced in: B. F. Dukore (ed.), *Bernard Shaw on Cinema*, Carbondale IL, 1997, p. 55, cf. pp. 53–4.

114 Robertson, *Hidden Cinema*, p. 30; I. Montagu, *The Political Censorship of Film*, London, 1929. I have been unable to trace the source of the quotation.

115 'The Battleship Potemkin', *The Times*, 12 November 1929, p. 14.

116 Robertson, *Hidden Cinema*, p. 30; B. Hogenkamp, *Deadly Parallels: Film and the Left in Britain, 1929–1939*, London, 1986, pp. 64, 83–90, 140.

117 L. Moussinac, *Sergei Eisenstein. An Investigation into His Films and Philosophy*, New York, 1970, p. 11.

118 The reception in France is covered in: K & L, pp. 249–57; Marshall, pp. 161–2.

119 G. Sadoul, *Le Cinéma français (1890–1962)*, Paris, 1962, p. 41.

120 Moussinac, pp. 10–11.

121 Y. Barna, *Eisenstein*, London and Bloomington IN, 1973, p. 111.

122 C. York, 'Studio News and Gossip East and West', *Photoplay Magazine*, October 1926, cited in: Marshall, pp. 187–8. The US reception is covered more fully in: Marshall, pp. 183–235.

123 Memo dated 15 October 1926, cited in: Marshall, pp. 189–90.

124 *New Yorker*, 18 December 1926, cited in: Marshall, p. 195.

125 P. Rotha, *The Film Till Now. A Survey of World Cinema*, revised edn, London, 1967, pp. 226–7.

126 F. Hardy (ed.), *Grierson on the Movies*, London and Boston MA, 1981, p. 180.

127 Hardy, p. 181.

128 C. Steinberg, *Reel Facts*, Harmondsworth, 1981, pp. 363–82.

129 Steinberg, pp. 383–4.

130 *Sight and Sound*, Winter 1961/2, pp. 10–11.

131 Steinberg, p. 369.
132 *Sight and Sound*, Autumn 1982, pp. 242–3.
133 *Sight and Sound*, December 1992, pp. 18–19.
134 Ibid., p. 31.
135 Sky Movies poll reported in *The Times*, 1 January 2000.

Further Reading

Eisenstein on *Potemkin*

Eisenstein's writings are now more easily accessible in English. His principal writings on *The Battleship Potemkin* may be found as follows:

S. M. Eisenstein, *Selected Works*:
  Vol. 1: Writings, 1922–34 (ed. and trans. R. Taylor), London and Bloomington IN, 1988 [abbreviated as *ESW1*], especially pp. 67–88, 90–3, 161–202, 280–95.
  Vol. 2: Towards A Theory of Montage (co-ed. M. Glenny and R. Taylor; trans. M. Glenny), London, 1991; paperback edn, 1994, especially pp. 227–49.
  Vol. 3: Writings, 1934–47 (ed. R. Taylor, trans. W. Powell), London, 1996, especially pp. 250–1.
  Vol. 4: Beyond the Stars. The Memoirs of Sergei Eisenstein (ed. R. Taylor, trans. W. Powell), London and Calcutta, India, 1995 [*ESW4*], especially pp. 143–82, 523–9, 797–8.
The Eisenstein Reader (ed. R. Taylor, trans. R. Taylor & W. Powell), London, 1998 [*ER*], especially pp. 60–72, 93–133, 145–59.
S. Eisenstein, *The Battleship Potemkin*, London, 1968
S. Eisenstein, *Nonindifferent Nature* (trans. H. Marshall), Cambridge, 1987, especially pp. 10–37.

Other Sources

J. Aumont, *Montage Eisenstein*, London & Bloomington IN, 1987.
Y. Barna, *Eisenstein*, London & Bloomington IN, 1973.
B. Beumers, 'Eisenstein's *The Battleship Potemkin*' in: S. Street and J. Forbes (eds), *Introduction to European Cinema*, Basingstoke, 2000.
D. Bordwell, *The Cinema of Eisenstein*, Chicago IL, 1993.
O. Bulgakowa, *Sergej Eisenstein, Eine Biographie*, Berlin 1998.
D. Gerould, 'Historical Simulation and Popular Entertainment. The *Potemkin* Mutiny from Reconstructed Newsreel to Black Sea Stunt Men', *Tulane Drama Review*, vol. 33, no. 2 (Summer 1989), pp. 161–84.

J. Goodwin, *Eisenstein, Cinema, and History*, Urbana IL, 1993.

R. Hough, *The 'Potemkin' Mutiny*, London, 1960.

J. Leyda and Z. Voynow, *Eisenstein at Work*, London and New York, 1982.

H. Marshall (ed.), *Sergei Eisenstein s 'The Battleship Potemkin'*, New York, 1978.

D. Mayer, *Sergei M. Eisenstein s 'Potemkin'. A Shot-by-Shot Presentation*, New York, 1972.

N. Swallow, *Eisenstein. A Documentary Portrait*, London, 1976; New York, 1977.

D. J. Wenden, '*Battleship Potemkin* – Film and Reality', in: K. R. M. Short (ed.), *Feature Films as History*, London, 1981, pp. 37–61.

Further Viewing

The Strike (Eisenstein, 1925)
The Battleship Potemkin (Eisenstein, 1925)
October (Eisenstein, 1927)
The Secret Life of Sergei Eisenstein (Gian-Carlo Bertelli, BFI, London, 1988)